MISS UNLIKELY

MISS UNLIKELY

From Farm Girl to Miss America

BETTY MAXWELL

BroadStreet
PUBLISHING

MISS UNLIKELY *From Farm Girl to Miss America*

978-1-4245-5780-6 (softcover)
978-1-4245-5781-3 (e-book)

Agent: Steve Ivey
Cover and interior: Garborg Design at GarborgDesign.com
Cover Photo: Matt Boyd Photography

Printed in the United States of America

19 20 21 22 23 5 4 3 2 1

This book is dedicated to anyone who has ever felt alone.
Anyone who has ever been told they're not good enough.
Anyone who has ever felt like a failure.
Anyone who feels lost or surrounded by darkness.

My hope is that this book gives you the confidence to love
and be yourself. This world needs you and your unique gifts.
God created you perfectly in his image
—you have a purpose on this earth.

I love you, and I believe in you!

CONTENTS

A NOTE FROM SPINNY

From the second I met Betty, I witnessed the inextinguishable light that lives within her. It is a light that inspires, guides, and shines brightly even through the darkest of times. Her story is one of unwavering tenacity.

As human beings in an imperfect world, we all face negativity, rejection, and criticism—some of us more than others. I've watched Betty overcome all of these things with a superhuman ability to focus on the positive and a relentless dedication to follow her heart. Despite the forces in life that try to hold us back from doing what we're truly meant to do, Betty has relied on her family and her faith to succeed, always trusting in God's plan for her.

I fell in love with Betty before she won Miss Georgia or Miss America, and I can say with complete confidence that through it all, she has remained just Betty: a normal girl from a small town in Georgia with a humble heart and down-to-earth spirit.

My hope is that you witness that same light and feel inspired to find your own. Let Betty's story be a testament that you can find the confidence in yourself to achieve your dreams. I know her well enough to know she'd tell you this: if she can do it, so can you.

—**Spencer Maxwell**, aka "Spinny"

FOREWORD
John Kirby

When I first heard the name Betty Cantrell, I knew I'd be hearing that name for years to come. I was in Winnipeg, Canada, at the time and on the set of DeVon Franklin's film *Breakthrough* to coach its star actress, Chrissy Metz. My associate, Nathan Nesbitt, told me a manager named Steve Ivey was on the line and wanted to discuss having me coach Betty, a former Miss America. Of course, the name Betty conjured up in my mind the image of a perfect, all-American housewife baking an apple pie.

Steve said he did his research on me and was aware of the many careers I had developed and launched and that I came highly recommended by a dear industry friend, Suzanne Niles. Hearing his Nashville sound took me back. It had been a while since I'd been down that road. Nashville is dear to me and a place where I had worked with so many wonderful country music artists.

Steve told me of Betty's singing career and suggested I check out her winning the 2016 Miss America pageant. When I watched the replay of her victory and heard her incredible voice sing, it dawned on me: of course, I remembered her. I remember having stopped in my tracks on the night she had won to listen to her extraordinary rendition of the operatic ballad "Tu, Tu Piccolo Iddio." The girl had amazing range and sang with emotional freedom and power that flowed out of her—not at all like Betty the homemaker I had imagined in a kitchen. Betty was the real deal: exceptional and fearless.

My growing up in a show-business family helped me build a strong work ethic, and I've always been fortunate to attract actors with the same discipline—those who want to dig in and truly do the work. This discipline is rare when so many young people today want to be famous without putting in the time to be exceptional.

I sent Betty an emotionally charged monologue to prepare for our first meeting, and when I had the opportunity to watch her perform it, it became clear to me that Betty's work ethic mirrored mine. I could see she was both willing to learn and willing to reveal so many parts of herself from within. She did a nice job, but I could tell she was still approaching it as if for the stage, and as we worked on my notes for her, we quickly developed a mutual trust and respect. She was honest in life, and her ability to bring that truth into her acting was going to put her way ahead of the game.

Our beginning to work together was a divine appointment, and we continue to work consistently around her busy schedule of raising up women to be the best they can be, encouraging strong values in honoring God, recording hair and makeup tutorials, and recording her YouTube series with her phenomenal husband. Together, they help young men and women meet the slings and arrows that life throws at them—from marriage to grief to following your dreams.

Betty's journey from the farm to the Miss America crown is quite inspiring, especially as she works with such discipline and continues to break new ground in her craft. It's exciting to walk with her as she journeys toward living out her dreams of acting in television, film, and under the bright lights of the Broadway stage. Her career continues to soar, and the industry continues to take notice.

You can take Betty out of the kitchen, but you can't take the heart of the farm girl out of Betty. That's what makes her so lovable. America's already fallen in love with her, and it would be highly unlikely for this American Miss—with her incomparable talent and beauty—to accomplish anything shy of captivating audiences from all around the world for years to come.

—John Kirby
Hollywood's premier acting coach and founder of The John Kirby Studio

Introduction

"We're down to the final three," announced Chris Harrison, the host of *The Bachelor* and *The Bachelorette*. It was Sunday, September 13, 2015, and the final night of the eighty-ninth Miss America pageant. I stood next to two incredible women on a stage inside Boardwalk Hall in Atlantic City, New Jersey, in front of a live audience of nearly 15,000 people with 7.9 million viewers watching from their homes. Chris was moments away from announcing 2016's Miss America. Only one of us would be crowned.

"You know what? Let me take a second here." He walked toward us, prolonging the already painful suspense. "How are we doing over here?" He placed his microphone in front of me.

"I'm having bad luck with my earrings tonight. One fell off just now and one at top fifteen. I just—I don't know what that means!" I couldn't help but laugh. I wouldn't be Betty if I hadn't had some kind of mishap.

"That's good luck. It's gotten you this far." Chris Harrison extended his microphone to Miss Tennessee and Miss South Carolina who stood next to me. "What could possibly be going through your minds at this moment?"

Both women expressed their gratitude and shared heartfelt, thoughtful responses. I couldn't help but wish I had said something meaningful too. Then cohost Brooke Burke asked Kira Kazantsev, Miss America 2015, how she was feeling. Kira reflected on her year and her excitement to pass on the crown, and Chris Harrison reminded the live audience and viewers of the prize: a $50,000 college scholarship. I huddled closely with Miss Tennessee and Miss South Carolina—our arms around each other and our eyes downcast in anticipation. It was finally time to announce the winner.

"Here she is . . .

Your new Miss America is . . .

Miss Georgia! Betty Cantrell!"

***

My life changed forever the moment Chris Harrison announced my name as Miss America 2016. People often ask me what went through my mind when he announced my state, and my answer is probably disappointing. The truth is that my mind went totally blank, and I lost control of my body. I started crying, and I almost fell to my knees on stage. I was just completely shocked to have heard my name. Miss South Carolina and Miss Tennessee both helped me stand up and get into position for the crowning.

It was a hectic, crazy moment. I felt completely overwhelmed with gratitude, and if you watch the YouTube video of these few minutes, you'll see that the only words I could utter were *thank you*. Thank you, God. Thank you, judges, for choosing me. The sash was draped over me, and the three rows of crystals that bordered the edges made it surprisingly heavy. Pageant crowns usually have an elastic band around the inside, and bobby pins are used to secure the elastic to your hair. But the crown was missing the elastic band, so Kira had to pin the crown to my head by poking bobby pins through little holes around the rim while I continued to sob and shake. Once I was able to think again, I thought, *What is happening to me right now?* I was handed the scepter, which had gorgeous, long-stemmed roses attached to it.

When the time came to take my first walk down the runway as Miss America, I hesitated for a moment. *Am I actually allowed to walk down this?* Only Miss America is allowed to walk down this runway, and it still hadn't sunk in that I had won! I touched the sash and felt the crown on my head and realized it was all really happening. I started to walk and wave at the crowd, and I vividly remember thinking, *My life will never be the same.* My hair kept getting caught in the stones of the sash, and the crown was barely attached to my head, but I didn't care. I saw my mom and dad at the end of the runway, where the organization allows the winner's parents to stand. When I reached them, I bent down and hugged them, thanking them and telling them I loved them.

I finished my walk down the runway, and the entire 2016 class of Miss America contestants mobbed me. We had our own hug-fest right there on stage. I think everyone who wins a pageant title worries she's going to see a picture or video from her crowning moment where someone in the background is rolling her eyes because you won, but I felt like my class was truly happy for me, and I'm so grateful for that. It truly is a sisterhood, and I know I would have been genuinely happy for any of my Miss America sisters to have won. Somehow, the crown stayed on my head through it all. Between the walk and the endless hugs, it absolutely should have fallen off. It may sound cheesy, but I like to imagine God's hand holding it in place for me. I certainly felt his presence that night.

After the pageant was over, I was ushered backstage and into a room to prepare for a press conference immediately following the pageant. Luckily, someone had elastic hair ties, so we cut them up and tied them together to create a makeshift band for the crown. The crown stayed like that throughout my entire year as Miss America and miraculously remained secure at every event.

A representative for the Miss America Organization was in the room with me as we haphazardly fastened my crown, and she asked, "Is there anything you need to tell me?" Prior to the pageant, the organization informed us that the winner would be taken into a room and asked if there was anything they needed to know. In essence, they want to know of any skeletons in your closet that they should be aware of so they can get ahead of potential bad press. I was so nervous about this question. I wracked my brain trying to think of anything I might be forgetting, but all that came to mind was an unpaid speeding ticket. The representative chuckled when I told her about it. Then I scanned my mind from as far back as I could remember and answered, "No, nothing else."

I was so excited to begin my year as Miss America. I knew I would be performing at events, making appearances, and traveling roughly 20,000 miles every month for the next year. What I didn't know was how that year would set into motion my lifelong dream of starting a career in singing and acting. I didn't know I would marry the man who had stood by my side during my year as Miss America. I didn't know I would go on to meet my incredible producer, record my first album, sign with a talent and modeling agency, celebrate my fairytale wedding, or buy my first home together with my new husband.

It sounds like a perfect, amazing life—and don't get me wrong, in many ways, it has been. I recognize how incredibly blessed I am. But there's so much about me and my journey you don't know, and I want to share the whole story with you—all of it—the awkward years and the not-so-perfect parts too. My year as Miss America was by far the toughest of my life, and without God, the man who would become my husband, and my family, I don't know how I would have made it.

As surprising as this may seem, I was never the little girl who dreamt of wearing the Miss America crown. The thought literally never even crossed my mind growing up. Ever since I was three years old, I wanted to be a singer and an actress, and to be honest, I didn't exactly know how I was going to make that happen. Maybe you have a similar story. Maybe you have a lifelong dream, and you wonder if you're ever going to get where you want to be. I'd like to think this book is not just an opportunity for you to get a behind-the-scenes look at the life of an unlikely Miss America; it's also a chance for me to share some of the lessons I've learned along the way. Lessons I learned from growing up on a farm. Lessons I learned from being raised in a strong family with a strong faith. Lessons I learned about boys, choices, disappointments, mentors, and so many other things.

My prayer for you is that when you finish reading this book, you are filled with hope for your future. We all come from so many different walks of life. We all have struggles and challenges. And we all have dreams. I want you to know that if a girl as unlikely as me can turn my dreams into a reality, you can too. You just need the right tools, people who love and support you, and a whole lot of faith.

CHAPTER 1

Family, Farm, and Faith

I was born on September 1, 1994, in Warner Robins, Georgia, a town located in the center of the state about one hundred miles south of Atlanta. According to my parents, Anastasia and Michael George Cantrell, I was born screaming. They tell me I was a notoriously loud baby and toddler—so much so that they would call me "Miss 60 D" since every sound I made was at a minimum volume of sixty decibels. I was simply incapable of whispering or using an "inside voice."

My parents named me Baciliky (pronounced "Vah-see-lee-key") after my grandmother on my mother's side of the family, which is full-blooded Greek. She passed away from stage four breast cancer when my mom was only eight years old, and my mom always said she would name her daughter after her. So that's me, and like my grandmother, I also go by the American nickname "Betty."

I have two siblings. My brother, "Mikey," was named after my dad and was two years old when I joined the family. Mikey was excited when I was born and called me *his* baby. He loved to hold and help take care of me. And as I grew older, we were instant playmates, spending our days entertaining each other. Then, when I was five, my mom became pregnant with a third child. She and my dad had decided not to find out the sex of the baby until the birth, so Mikey and I took bets on whether the baby would be a girl or a boy. I, of course, was hoping for a sister, and Mikey wanted a brother. It was clearly more of a battle of the sexes for the household majority, and the girls won! Sophia was born, and because she was so much younger than us, Mikey and I both felt like she was *our* baby.

I was blessed with two incredible parents, both of whom are strikingly beautiful. My dad's fair skin and strawberry blonde hair are evidence of his Irish heritage. He has a square, Germanic jaw, and his physique reveals his past as a former bodybuilder. My mom is Greek and has the hallmark olive skin and thick, dark chestnut hair. Her smile radiates warmth. Whenever my friends met my parents for the first time, they would always comment on my parents' good looks. They were also smart and driven. They owned a successful physical therapy practice, renting office space early on in their business and later building the Cantrell Center in Warner Robins.

Growing up, my dad was the strict disciplinarian, and my siblings and I had a healthy fear of him, never wanting to disappoint him or get into trouble. Whenever one of us kids was upset over something, he would say, "There are only two ways to go through life: happy or sad. So, what's it gonna be?"

Reluctantly, we'd answer, "Happy."

"Okay," he'd say. "Then be happy, or I'll give you something to cry about."

He was a no-nonsense parent and never coddled us. At the same time, though, he was impulsive, fun, and always the life of the party. He loved to hunt and tend the 675-acre farm we lived on. He built deer stands and laid trails throughout the woods that he named after us: Mike Street, Betty Lane, and Sophia Island. He'd also name them after characters that appeared on *The Andy Griffith Show*, like Andy Griffith, Opie, Goober, and Gomer. He planted food plots for the dove and deer hunting seasons, and he taught us how to hunt, skin, and clean deer, doves, and rabbits. We were always helping Dad with chores around the farm. If he wasn't on the tractor, we were. And there was no such thing as "man's work" according to my dad. Sophia and I were just as involved with the manual labor of the property as Mikey was, and I am so grateful that my dad gave us the same amount of responsibility and trust with farm work.

My mom, Anastasia, goes by Tassie, and she's known for her kindness and her beauty. She was extremely cautious, prone to worry, and endearingly overprotective—as so many good moms are. She was also careful and smart, and she'd think through things from every angle before making a decision. I couldn't simply go to the movies with friends; she had to know who was going, if there was going to be an adult present, which movie it was, how long the movie ran, and at least fifteen other things. She was also a disciplinarian, but we never took her as seriously as we did Dad. But if Mom was truly upset, we knew we must have done something bad because she was always more of the peacemaker. And like many mothers, she was our dedicated taxi driver. She took us to school and to the majority of our extracurricular activities—dance classes, ballet recitals, soccer practice, musical theater performances and rehearsals, Boy Scouts, Brownies, tee ball, and gymnastics—somehow managing to balance it all with her own career. Looking back, I can only imagine how hard it must have been to coordinate schedules for three kids, and I can't give her enough praise for that.

My parents purchased our farm in Fort Valley, Georgia, a rural town about twenty miles west of Warner Robins, when I was a year old, and it was a huge investment given its size. Until they could pay off the property and build their dream home, they decided to purchase a double-wide trailer for our family to live in temporarily. Later, they built a barn as well as a new physical therapy practice, which further delayed the building of our home. So, what was meant to be a temporary solution ended up being the home I lived in my entire childhood until I left for college.

The farm is in the middle of nowhere. We didn't have neighbors nearby for me to compare my house to, so our double-wide trailer never bothered me. I never felt like "trailer trash" or weird, poor, or lesser than my friends. The farm—our own huge playground where we had the freedom to explore, imagine, and learn—more than made up for the fact that we lived in a trailer.

As I said, the farm is made up of a vast 675 acres. The dirt driveway stretches for three miles and is a straight shot to the house. As you're nearing the house, the driveway is lined on either side by row after row of pecan trees and then the orchard ends at a clearing. Dead center in the clearing sat our double-wide trailer (now replaced by a permanent home). A large barn stood to the left of our trailer, and to the right was a second trailer. Woods surround the entire property on all sides with trails snaking their way through the dense trees.

I absolutely loved growing up on the farm; it truly was the best part of my childhood. I was always outside getting dirty and experiencing things that the world couldn't teach me. It's so easy nowadays for families to tune each other out and spend their time together just scrolling through their phones or staring at devices. But my parents were intentional about giving us a love for the outdoors and maintaining closeness within our family. My dad helped us build our beloved treehouse where I hosted tea parties. My mom would prepare tea for me, and my dad would join me and eat the jelly beans I served my guests. Mikey, Sophia, and I explored the extensive trails that my father created on our golf cart or four-wheeler, and we memorized every square foot of the land that became so much a part of who we are.

My dad's mother, Lottie Cantrell, also lived on the farm in the second double-wide trailer that sat to the right of ours. She was our "Omi," a nickname coined by Mikey that's derived from the German word for grandma. We loved having her nearby. Omi had grown up in Germany during World War II. She was proper, smart, and sophisticated, and she'd jokingly refer to me as "James" whenever I drove her around the property in our golf cart. "Take me to the barn, James," she'd say in her fancy accent, and I'd listen obediently as if I were her driver. Though she passed away when I was only twelve, I always held so much respect for her and felt her loss once she was gone.

As far as childhoods go, ours was pretty sheltered. The expanse of our property naturally isolated us, and my parents were much stricter than most. We didn't even have cable television. Instead, we watched DVDs of old shows like *The Andy Griffith Show*, *Gilligan's Island*, and *The Wild Wild West*. My parents were careful about what we watched, who we played with, and how we spent our time. While they gave us free reign on the farm to explore and run free, they were ever present in activities off the farm. I'll never forget my first sleepover with my best friend, Natalie, when I was five. Before my mother would ever allow me to go, she had to get to know Natalie's parents first. Finally, once she felt confident in their devout Catholic faith, she said I could spend the night but with one stipulation: that she spent the night too. Thankfully, at five years old, I didn't mind much, but looking back on it, I can't help but laugh at my mom's fierce protection.

We were a close family, and given our tight living quarters, we had—and were allowed—very little privacy. There were times when I just wanted to go to my room, but I couldn't because we were having family time. I'd often ask my parents why my friends could have televisions in their rooms but I couldn't. Their response never wavered or changed: "We do things as a family." Nights and weekends usually meant we were watching movies together or playing Andy Griffith Trivia. We played that board game nonstop, and it was always our goal as kids to beat Dad (I think all three of us have successfully beaten him at least once by now). Mornings were spent eating cereal together while watching an episode of *The Andy Griffith Show*, and we always ate dinner as a family. I have very few childhood memories, if any, where I was alone or isolated. My parents and siblings were always present, always close.

Every Sunday, we'd pile into the car and head to the Holy Cross Greek Orthodox Church in Macon, which was a forty-five-minute drive from our house. Attending church was always important to our family. Holy Cross wasn't a huge church by any means. There were only around fifty people in the pews on any given Sunday. The Greek Orthodox church doesn't exactly appeal to the masses because it's steeped in tradition and requires a lot of its parishioners. But our family loved this faith tradition, and every Sunday we'd put on our "Sunday best," which meant suits for my dad and Mikey and dresses for my mom, Sophia, and me. Some Sunday mornings, my parents would take us to Krispy Kreme for donuts before church. We would stand with our faces pressed against the glass window and watch as the donuts moved down the conveyor belts and were bathed in sugary glaze. This was a big deal for us as kids because in the Greek Orthodox church, you fasted on Sunday mornings before taking communion. And while my parents always modeled this sacrifice and later expected it of us, they also let us be kids when we were younger.

At Holy Cross, my brother was an altar boy, and our family sang in the choir—so much so that people called us the Von Trapp family singers, the real-life family that the movie *The Sound of Music* was based on. And if we couldn't make it to church for whatever reason, that usually meant there was no choir. This was where my love for music and singing began. Keep in mind, we sang old, traditional Byzantine hymns in Greek—not the popular praise and worship music you hear in many churches today.

As early as three years old, I remember longing to become a singer. This was right around the time I stopped sucking my thumb. My dad would tell me, "It was like there was music bottled up behind your thumb." So, when I kicked my thumb habit, my parents discovered that I could actually sing. And once I started, I couldn't stop! But when they would encourage me to sing in church, I never wanted to. I didn't like the spotlight or singing in front of our small church or for people I knew well. It made me nervous, but thankfully, it was something I was forced to grow out of.

Faith was the foundation of our family. From as early as I can remember, my parents instilled in us a love for God and a longing to serve him. They looked for ways to teach us and mold us. At one point, our parents decided we should have a family Bible study every morning at 5:00 a.m. to read Scripture together. Unfortunately, this stint didn't last long because Mikey, Sophia, and I kept falling asleep at the table. I dreaded those early morning Bible studies at the time, but looking back, those mornings sent a meaningful message to me and my siblings: faith was a priority. My parents were so intentional about encouraging a deep faith in us—and with remarkable success because mine has never wavered. Without a strong foundation in Christ, I don't know who I would be today.

My family, our farm, and my faith all had such a lasting impact on me. My parents instilled in me a profound gratitude for spending time with family—something that I want to nurture with my own kids someday. Our beautiful farm gave me a love for nature and the outdoors. It fed my imagination and gave me a sense of adventure and exploration that is so much a part of who I am. And my faith helped create the foundation for my values and beliefs. I would be nothing without my faith in God. So, yes, my family, our farm, and my faith are like the soundtrack of my entire childhood. Those three things played on through the good and the bad, the happy and the sad, and I consider them some of my greatest gifts from God. I can honestly say that they are what made me the down-to-earth, grounded person I am today.

CHAPTER 2

A Social Butterfly with a Flair for Drama

Just before I started elementary school, I had to be tested to see if I was academically ready. Since my birthday falls in September and is close to the cutoff for kindergarten registration, my test results would determine if I could start school then or if I'd need to wait another year. Fortunately, I knew my shapes and colors and passed the test, so my parents enrolled me in the same private Catholic school that Mikey attended. Every Wednesday morning, the entire school would go to mass at the church adjacent to the school. Even though we were a devout Greek Orthodox family, my Catholic school environment never caused me to question my own beliefs. That piece of my identity has thankfully always been strong.

From the time I could talk and express myself, I had a flair for drama. This side of me really came out once I entered school and was surrounded by friends—and especially boys. Even at six years old, I had a crush on a boy named Dominic in my kindergarten class. Unfortunately, another girl in my class liked him too. In my mind, my life was a movie, complete with a villain, a hero, and a heroine: me! That meant I absolutely, positively could not be friends with this girl. She was my rival. My enemy. But, as fate would have it, Dominic moved away in second grade, so that girl who had been trying to come between us? Well, we became immediate friends, of course.

My dramatic side would also come out during car rides home from school with my mom and Mikey. My mom would ask us about our day, and our answers were pretty telling of our personalities.

"It was fine. Just a normal day," Mikey would say.

But when it was my turn, I gave my mom a full rundown, which usually sounded something like this: "Mom, you're never gonna believe this, but Dominic smiled at me today! And my teacher was out sick, so we had a substitute. Natalie and I got to the swing set first at recess yesterday, but today we had to have indoor recess because it was raining. I had pizza for lunch, and there was spinach in it! It was so gross. Oh, and I was chosen to sing the solo at Mass next Wednesday!"

For me, school was an opportunity to socialize and hang out with friends. I was more of a social butterfly than a serious student. But I always tried really hard, and if I underperformed, I would go to great lengths to convince my parents otherwise. I never wanted to "bother" them with bad grades. My school's policy for poor grades was that you had to take the assignment home, have a parent sign it, and then return it to the teacher to prove your parent had seen the grade.

In second grade, I was sent home with a red letter F at the top of one of my papers. I shoved the paper into my backpack and immediately began sweating over how I was going to present it to my parents.

Then it hit me: I could simply forge my mom's signature at the top and turn it in the next day. I wouldn't even have to worry her with it. Brilliant! But this being my first experience with this sort of thing, I didn't think to sign my mom's first and last name. No. Instead, I signed "Mom" in black ink. Of course, my teacher sent the assignment back home with me, and I had to break the news to my parents.

I got in so much trouble, and you would have thought I'd learned my lesson. But for some reason, I tried to get away with it a second time on a different assignment! This time I knew to write my mom's actual name. So, I wrote "Tassie" next to the circled letter C at the top of the paper. Only, instead of writing in cursive, I wrote it in print. Again, my teacher sent the assignment back home. I was in double trouble because not only had I received a low grade, but I had also lied about it and forged my mom's signature. I got a whippin' and was put on what my parents called "restriction." This meant if I wasn't at school, I was in my room. Not hanging out with the family, not watching movies in the evening, not attending sleepovers, and not having friends over. Nothing.

I was a bad liar and clearly lacked attention to detail. It wasn't that I was trying to get away with something or avoid consequences; I just didn't want to disappoint my parents. I was an average student who struggled with grades, and that was embarrassing for me. I desperately wanted to make my parents and Omi proud of me. But by the time I reached third grade, I wasn't performing well.

At the beginning of each day, my third-grade teacher would write a list of books we needed for the first part of the day on the whiteboard, and then she'd set a timer for two minutes. In that time, we were supposed to retrieve the books from our cubbies at the back of the classroom and return to our seats. I would squint and strain to see the yellow dry-erase marker my teacher loved to write with, but when I couldn't make out the words, I'd randomly grab books from my cubby and hope for the best. I didn't know something was wrong with my vision; I just figured other people were better at seeing than me. Thankfully, my teacher caught on and sent a note home asking my parents to have my eyes checked to see if I needed glasses. And sure enough, I did!

I wasn't worried or embarrassed about having to get glasses. I was a confident kid. Besides, I had seen an episode of *Arthur* on PBS where Arthur gets his first pair of glasses. He was afraid he was going to be teased or bullied for having to wear them, but his classmates thought they were cool, and it turned out that it was okay to be different. *This is going to be fine*, I thought.

When I wore them to school for the first time, I walked in with my head held high, fully expecting to get compliments like Arthur had. Maybe a "Cool glasses!" or "You look awesome!" But no one even noticed. It was like any other day at school, which was a huge let down. Then, when my best friend Natalie got glasses and wore them to school for the first time, everyone noticed and made a big deal about it. Even the teacher brought it to our class's attention. *You've gotta be kidding me!* I thought. *This is so unfair!* Natalie was a perfect student who made straight As and was loved by our teachers. She was my best friend, and I loved her too, but I was also jealous of her. To this day, she is still one of my closest friends and was a bridesmaid in my wedding, but as a kid I so desperately wanted to be like her.

When Natalie started ballet, I naturally wanted to start ballet too. I ended up loving it and really got into it. Around the time I was ten, a new ballet studio opened up across the street from the Cantrell Center, my parents' physical therapy practice. This studio was supposed to be the ballet studio for serious, aspiring professional ballerinas, so both Natalie and I started dancing there. The lady who owned it was very strict, and I responded well to her teaching style because it was similar to my parents' discipline. I was the tallest girl in the class and not exactly the most flexible, but I tried so, so hard to keep up with the other girls—some of whom were homeschooled so they'd have more time for ballet. I'd practice my pliés, pirouettes, and arabesques in my front yard, and from her front porch, Omi would say, "You need to be more fluid" or "Nice technique, Betty!"

If I wasn't in ballet class after school, I was at tennis lessons. Omi had coerced my siblings and me to start playing tennis once we turned four years old, and we had lessons after school at least three days a week. Omi would pick us up in her old, red Mercedes convertible and drive us to our lessons, and on warm days, she'd put the top down. Of course, that was the coolest thing ever to us.

She'd watch our lessons and then critique us afterward, telling us what we did well and what we needed to work on. She'd also make us eat bananas because, according to Omi, they made us play better. I've always hated bananas and still do to this day, but I never gave her any lip about it because if there was one person I was not going to talk back to, it was Omi. She was a strong believer in single player sports and despised team sports. In her thick, German accent she would say, "If you're going to fail, you're going to fail on your own. If you're going to win, you're going to win on your own. You don't need anybody else."

I hated tennis, even though I was pretty good at it. I played U.S. tournaments and usually placed well. But I'd complain to my mom and ask, "How long do I have to do this? I hate tennis."

"Well, your Omi wants you to play."

"So do I have to play tennis forever?" I'd whine.

"You just need to keep playing tennis for as long as Omi wants you to play tennis," she'd reply. I eventually read between the lines, understanding that as long as Omi was alive, I was expected to play tennis.

During our summer breaks, we had a lot of responsibilities on the farm. Our parents worked, so they would leave a list of chores for us to complete. And these weren't your ordinary "make your bed, feed the dog, and clean your room" type of chores. The list would include things like clean the house, lay pine straw, water all the plants inside and outside, and clean the pool. It was almost entirely manual labor, and our parents made sure we knew how to do these kinds of tasks ourselves. Our friends would often ask if we could hang out, but we weren't allowed to because we had chores or summer reading to do. My parents used this time to instill a strong work ethic in us. Of course, I didn't like it, but because of it, I now understand the importance and value of getting stuff done.

One of our many chores was to feed and care for the animals. I'm not exaggerating when I say we had a menagerie of pets. We always had at least one Great Dane among other hunting dogs, like Beagles, Bluetick Hounds, and English Setters. Dad considered little dogs "useless" and wouldn't allow us to have one. We had guinea hens, chickens, pygmy goats, and an occasional chipmunk or squirrel. We even had a few pigeons that my dad thought he could train to be messengers, but they just flew away and never came back. Mikey was fascinated with snakes and would set traps to catch them for pets. Then he'd put them in the bathtub and feed them mice or rats. We'd stand in the bathroom and watch, and it never once scared me. It was simply part of growing up on a farm.

Around age seven, we rescued an abandoned baby deer, and I named her Annie. My parents made me wake up early every morning to feed her milk from a bottle. My dad has a photo hanging in his office of me feeding Annie one morning, standing outside in my underwear—half asleep and holding a bottle up to Annie's mouth. I didn't love having to wake up so early, but my parents let me know that Annie was my responsibility, and they weren't going to feed her for me.

Mikey once caught a possum that was foaming at the mouth. We thought it was rabid, but by the next morning, it had given birth. My brother and I each decided to name a baby possum. I named mine Curly Erin Hiss. Curly came from his prehensile tail. Miss Erin at the Cantrell Center was my favorite employee, so I was sure to include her in his name. And he earned the name Hiss for hissing all the time. We have pictures of him sitting on my head, hanging off my finger from his tail, and lying in my hair. Once the baby possums got big, we released them back into the wild.

For Easter one year, my dad brought home ducks from our local Tractor Supply store for Sophia and me. The store would dye the eggs, so that when they hatched, the feathers of the ducklings were a fun, bright color. My duck had bright green feathers, and the feathers of Sophia's duck were a vibrant orange. Once they molted, the color disappeared, and their normal adult feathers grew in. They were adorable and sweet as ducklings, but once they were grown, they were terribly mean. They would chase us whenever we went outside. I'm telling you, it's like they plotted their attack and just waited for us to leave the house. Then one Christmas, we ate them for dinner. This was farm life. We loved our animals, but we also understood that some of them would end up on our table.

By far, my favorite pet growing up was a baby fox named Foxy. After a major thunderstorm one day, Foxy was separated from his mom, so we adopted him. (I now know it's actually illegal to rescue wild animals in most states without a permit. Yikes!) I wanted to name him Todd from the Disney movie *The Fox and the Hound*, but that name just wouldn't stick. So Foxy it was. He was painfully cute. He fit in the palm of our hands, and his fur was silky soft. At first, he would hiss and nip at us. He was wild, after all, and not used to humans. As he grew up, his fur became coarse, but he loved to cuddle with us—especially with our Great Dane, Otis. We'd often have to search for him in the house because he liked to be somewhere in a dark corner, and he usually hid under the couch or a dresser. Eventually, we released him back into the woods. For a few months after that, we'd see him running around the property, far enough from the house to keep his distance but close enough that we could easily see him and recognize him. I liked to think that was his way of checking in on us and saying "hello."

As young kids, we spent nearly all of our time outside. Mikey and I were close in age and constantly wrestled around. We were always trying to think of new things to do, and we'd often dare each other to do silly—sometimes stupid—things. One day, Mikey and I were sitting on the front porch and feeling bored from our usual activities of playing in the treehouse and chasing each other along the trails when Mikey said, "Hey, I dare you to pick a leaf off one of the pecan trees and eat it."

"You do it first," I said.

"No. I dared you first. Are you too scared?" he taunted me.

We went back and forth for a minute before I said, "Okay, whatever. I'll do it. I don't care." I ran to the orchard, plucked a leaf off one of the trees, and ate it. It was disgusting—bitter, kinda crunchy, and really hard to swallow—exactly what you might imagine a leaf would taste like. But the last thing I was going to do was let Mikey win a bet or call me a chicken.

Later that day, Mikey and I retold the story to my mom. He couldn't believe I had actually eaten it.

"Yeah, I ate a leaf!" I said proudly.

"You did what?" my mom asked.

"What's the big deal?" I asked. "It's like eating vegetables."

"Betty, those trees were just sprayed with chemicals for bugs!"

She was freaking out in her worrisome way and was ready to call poison control, but my dad calmed her down: "She's going to be fine. Don't worry. We'll keep an eye on her." And he was right; nothing happened.

As strict and protective as our parents were, they gave us so much freedom on our farm. We explored the woods, climbed trees, and found countless animals to call our own. From that experience, not only did I gain a profound appreciation for wildlife and nature, but I can also name just about every kind of lizard, snake, and bird native to the state of Georgia. And although our parents' love for us was always evident, they never spoiled us. They taught us from an early age to work and to work hard. They certainly could have spoiled us. By this time in their careers, they were earning a solid, steady income. They could have hired professional help to tend the farm, but they made sure we worked every single day and did things that most kids never have to do.

At the time, I didn't understand their intentionality, and I didn't exactly appreciate having to work so hard. But looking back, I'm so grateful for the work ethic that caring for animals and tending the farm instilled in me. I learned the importance of working hard in everything that I do—whether that's as an average ballet dancer or a strong tennis player who's just playing to please my Omi. My elementary years may not have been all that conventional, but they laid a foundation of hard work and responsibility that has stuck with me throughout my life.

CHAPTER 3

Growing Pains

Every September around Labor Day, which also happens to be my birthday, our family hosted a dove shoot on our farm. It was a huge celebration to kick off the opening of dove season in Georgia. My dad would invite all of his hunting buddies and friends to our farm, and it wasn't unusual for up to two hundred men to show up.

My dad would carefully prepare a special area on the property that we called the dove field, which was about thirty acres of land. Starting in the spring and throughout the summer, we'd plant sunflowers, soybeans, or wheat to attract the doves. Mikey and I would sometimes help by plowing and burning the fields just before the season began. Burning the field got rid of all the brush but left seeds behind for the doves to eat. Since doves are creatures of habit, they return to land where they know they can find food.

The hunters would set up all around the field with their gear: guns, folding chairs, bags of bullets, and some would bring their bird dogs too. When we were little, Mikey, Sophia, and I served as Dad's bird dogs. Whenever he shot a dove, we would run out into the field, find it, and retrieve it. Our annual dove shoot was especially exciting because there were so many men, so my brother, sister, and I would run through the fields, finding the doves and bringing them back to whomever had shot them. My dad and all the men included us in the event, and I never felt like they were annoyed with us or wished we weren't there. They would thank us for our help and talk to us as if we were one of the adults.

Then, once the shoot was over, my dad and all his buddies would carry their doves to picnic tables set up just outside the barn, and there they'd clean the birds. It was a messy scene, as you can imagine. They'd pull the feathers off the bird, remove the breast, throw away the innards and remains in giant trash bags, and set the breast meat aside to cook later. This never grossed me out, and I honestly never felt sorry for the doves. I know how that may sound, but this was farm life. To me, the doves were food. I understood we'd be eating them for dinner at some point.

After everyone was finished cleaning their doves, we would all hang out together, talking and eating. And because the shoot was usually on or around my birthday, my parents would call everyone to the barn where they'd have a giant birthday cake waiting for me. Everyone would sing "Happy Birthday," and, grinning ear to ear, I'd blow out the candles. Then we'd pass out cake to everyone and have the biggest birthday party ever. For several years, I thought this entire event was put on just to celebrate my birthday! I figured I must have been the coolest kid ever for all of these people to show up just for me. Never mind the fact that they were mostly men and my dad's friends. This was my big day. I eventually realized that this was pure coincidence, of course, but it's such a fun memory of my childhood.

Once I was in middle school, I started inviting my friends to the dove shoot too. I'd have my birthday party during the day while my dad and his buddies did their thing. Since the dove field ran alongside our driveway, I'd have to warn my friends and their moms who were dropping them off to honk as they drove toward the house to make sure the shooters knew a car was coming through. It made many of my friends and their moms nervous, and they would freak out at the sight of a hundred men pointing guns in the air. "It's fine," I'd assure them. "You're not gonna get shot." We always had the best time at the annual dove shoot, and as far as birthday traditions go, I think mine was pretty awesome.

Most people look back on their middle-school years as the most awkward years of their lives. And like most young teenagers, I went through an awkward stage too. Let me tell you: It. Was. Rough. I had a big gap between my two front teeth and terrible acne. I wasn't allowed to wear makeup, so I couldn't do anything to even try to hide my breakouts. And I had no idea what to do with my hair other than brush it. Then, suddenly it was like one day I woke up with the largest chest of all the girls in my ballet class, most of whom were still flat-chested and petite. So not only was I the tallest girl in class, but now my chest also made me stand out even more.

Needless to say, I didn't consider myself pretty, and I certainly wasn't confident about my body. I don't know many middle-school girls—or boys, for that matter—who are. I sometimes felt insecure, but all of my friends felt the same way, so we were in it together. I never felt alone in the struggle, and thankfully, my body image wasn't something I thought about constantly or obsessed over. It was just something I accepted about myself. It was the reality of this stage in my life, and I knew it would eventually pass. We were all weird and awkward. Keep in mind that this was before the days of Instagram, which is now an ever-present comparison game for young girls who are measuring themselves against flawless, airbrushed models. I'm so thankful I didn't have to navigate that pressure at that stage of my life.

As far as academics went, my lack of interest in school didn't improve in middle school either. My grades for the most part continued to be average. Aside from ballet, I was focused on which boys liked me and what they thought about me. And even though I knew I wasn't allowed to date until high school, I would endlessly write in my diary about boys—boys I liked, boys I thought I might like at some point, boys I no longer liked. My entire Catholic middle-school class was made up of only fifteen kids, six of whom were boys, so I didn't exactly have a ton of boys to write about! Billy was one of those boys. I had a huge crush on him and his bright red hair. I wanted so desperately for him to like me because I just knew we were destined for each other.

My social life in and outside of school was the most important thing to me. Seeing my friends at school, at extracurricular activities, or hanging out with them at my house fed my extroverted personality. But my parents' protection was still just as evident as it had been during elementary school. If there was a school dance or event, I wasn't allowed to go unless my mom or dad went with me. Being dropped off at a movie or the mall with friends was out of the question, and there were many times I opted not to go places because I didn't want my mom or dad tagging along. So, most of the time, friends would just come to my house to hang out. There, my parents could keep an eye on all of us and knew we were safe and not getting into trouble. And I didn't mind it so much at the time. My friends loved the farm because it was different from what they were used to. We would swim when the weather was warm, run around exploring the farm, and just sit inside and talk.

Then when I was in seventh grade, the hardest of my middle-school years, my Omi passed away. She had been a smoker for forty years, and even though she quit at the age of seventy-three, she had contracted emphysema, and her kidneys gradually started to fail. The night she passed, my parents had dropped off Mikey, Sophia, and me at the home of a family friend while they went to the hospital to be with Omi. In the middle of the night, my parents came into the room where we were sleeping, woke us up, and broke the news. I was, of course, devastated.

Omi had been a constant presence in my life, and she was supportive of everything my siblings and I did. And she wasn't just present—she was in it with us, taking us to practices, cheering us on, giving us advice. I looked up to her with such respect and awe. She was always so put together. She'd have someone come to the house to do her nails and hair, which was never gray. Whether it was her fancy car, her tasteful, expensive jewelry, the air of sophistication with which she carried herself, or the fact that she spoke seven languages, all of it made up the wonder and beauty of my Omi. And I felt her loss in such a huge way. I only knew her for twelve years, but that felt like forever to me.

Omi loved to listen to me sing, and at her funeral, our whole family expected me to sing in her honor. Because of all the emotions from those past few days, I just didn't feel up to it. But my dad, the disciplinarian, said, "You are going to get up there and sing for your Omi." So I did. Omi had taught me how to sing "Silent Night" in

German, so I sang the song in both English and German. They were the hardest songs I've ever had to get through, and I cried throughout both renditions. My Omi had a remarkable impact on my life. Losing her was the first time I realized how short life is and how important it is to not take people for granted, especially the ones who love and care about you deeply.

And so, with Omi's death I also said goodbye to tennis once and for all. I played for one more year, through eighth grade, but I didn't continue in high school. I was still doing ballet at the same studio and enjoying it—although I think somewhere deep down, I knew it would not be for much longer. Then, at the encouragement of my mom, I began taking classical voice lessons. I had been singing all of my life in church, in the car, and at home, and everyone always said I should take voice lessons. But I had always been too busy with other activities or too young.

Natalie's older sister was a talented singer with a beautiful voice, and she recommended I take lessons from Nadine Cheek at Wesleyan College. Nadine didn't typically train fourteen-year-olds like myself, so I had to audition for her. Thankfully, she took me on as a student despite my age. From then on through high school, my mom would drive me forty-five minutes one way to Wesleyan twice a week for one-hour lessons with Nadine. She was the head of the vocal department, and I felt mature to be taking voice lessons at a college! She was a fantastic instructor and worked so well with me, especially considering how young I was. I credit my strong foundation in opera singing to those first few years of training with Nadine.

As hard and awkward as those middle school years were, I had finally found my thing—music, specifically singing and performing—and I loved it. It was the thing I enjoyed doing more than anything else. I couldn't get enough of it, soaking up all the learning and training and absolutely loving the feeling of using my voice to make music. And I started getting noticed because of it. I enjoyed people's compliments because they gave me the confidence to start believing in myself and in my talent. I began to believe that this was a gift God had given me and something I might be able to do when I grew up. God hadn't created me to play tennis or given me the flexibility of a professional ballerina. But he had given me other strengths and talents—ones that were unique to me, Betty Cantrell. He made me for a reason, and I was excited to chase the dreams he had planted in my heart.

CHAPTER 4

There's No Place Like Theatre

No one in the history of orthodontic work could have possibly been more excited to get braces than I was. It was the summer before my freshman year of high school, and I could not wait to get the gap between my front teeth corrected. I thought getting braces would be a lot like getting glasses: people would make a big deal about them, and the braces would add something new to my persona. But as soon as they were glued to my teeth, I thought, *These are the worst! Why was I excited about this?* My mouth and jaws ached, and the metal now covering my teeth made brushing and flossing nearly impossible—not that I flossed very often, if I'm being completely honest. But, most importantly, they did not look cute. I wanted them off from day one.

Then, as if starting high school with braces wasn't enough to deal with, Natalie and her family decided she would be home-schooled starting her freshman year so she could concentrate on ballet. I was heartbroken, and as much as I wanted to be mad at her, I knew that was unfair. Besides, I was happy my best friend was chasing her dream, even if that meant I was going to have to enter Mount de Sales High School all by myself. A few of my classmates from middle school would be going to the Catholic private school too, but Natalie was my very best friend. We had been inseparable for years, and just the thought of having to walk through those doors on the first day without her by my side made my heart race.

Thankfully, I still saw Natalie every day at ballet, and we spent our weekends together attending ballet competitions, so we'd catch up nearly every day. But to say I missed her during the school day would be an understatement. I struggled with finding my place initially. Natalie and I hadn't been part of a big group of friends or a clique, and I wasn't the type of person who could easily go out and make friends. It was out of my comfort zone. And although I can talk to just about anybody now, back then it was a real struggle for me. Even today I only have a few best friends, and I'm perfectly okay with that. But when you are a freshman in high school, well, the more friends you have, the cooler you seem.

I remember my first day of school at Mount de Sales like it was yesterday. I was so nervous about what everyone else would think of me and so terrified about where to go and what to do that I didn't even eat lunch. I was afraid I would eat in the wrong place or stand in the wrong line. So many things could go wrong, so I just stood outside the cafeteria by myself, leaning against a pole. As I stood there with my head down, I suddenly heard some of my older brother's friends, who I'd known forever, call out to me: "Betty! Come sit with us!"

Hesitantly, I walked over and sat next to them on the steps outside the cafeteria. In just a moment, I had gone from being a lonely freshman to a freshman who was sitting with cool upperclassmen! Their kindness that day was something I'll never forget, and something I'm still grateful for to this day.

When Mount de Sales announced auditions for the fall, one-act play, I wondered if this could be my new thing at school. I loved singing, and my voice lessons at Wesleyan were helping to build my confidence. I had also always dreamed of acting, so I decided to audition. The play was *Wiley and the Hairy Man*, which only had two main characters. I auditioned without any expectations of landing a role as those usually went to upperclassmen. I read a few quick lines from a script, and just like that my audition was over. I was placed in the ensemble, which meant I was kind of in the background, but I didn't mind it in the least. My parents had raised me to handle disappointment and criticism with grace. What mattered to them was that I give my very best and feel proud of myself no matter what.

As soon as rehearsals began for the show, I knew I was in love. I had been bitten by the acting bug and in a big way. I had fun at the practices after school, which forced me to branch out and make new friends. I loved the heat from standing under the stage lights, the adrenaline rushing through my veins as the curtain parted open, and the excitement from the full audience buzzing with anticipation. Performing was even more fun than I had ever imagined it would be. I couldn't get enough of it. We also got to perform our one-act plays at regional and state competitions, and the thrill of competing against other high schools was indescribable. After the play wrapped, I couldn't wait for the spring semester to try out for the musical.

By the time the spring semester came around, I had developed an enormous crush on a boy named Myles, who I thought was so nice and so cute. It didn't matter that we had never spoken or hardly ever made eye contact. Never in a million years did I think he would notice me. I had braces and glasses. I still wasn't allowed to wear makeup, and I didn't know how to style my hair.

One day at school, Myles' friends came up to me and said, "It's going down today!" But when I asked what that meant, they just repeated themselves saying, "It's going down!" I had no idea what they were talking about, so I thought, *Whatever,* and went about my day. Myles and I had religion class together, and during class that day, he kept whispering to his friends and laughing. I was certain they were making fun of me since they all knew I had a huge crush on him. I shrunk in my chair—*so* completely embarrassed.

I was walking out of my last class when Myles caught up to me in the hall and stopped me. This was it. This was the moment I would find out what was going down.

"Hey Betty, do you want to be my girlfriend?" he asked.

Oh my gosh, I thought, *Myles just asked me to be his girlfriend!* I immediately said yes, but I had never had a boyfriend. I was clueless as to what that even meant or what it required of me. And I'm pretty sure that poor Myles didn't either. When my mom picked me up from play practice that day, I jumped into her car and couldn't tell her the news fast enough: "Mom! Guess what?! Myles asked me to be his girlfriend!"

Despite my best efforts to convince my parents I needed a cell phone, I wouldn't get one until I was seventeen, and not having a cell phone really complicated my relationship (if you can even call it that) with Myles. I felt so lame for not having a phone and would constantly complain about it to my mom: "But Mom, what if you're late picking me up from school? How am I going to call you? What if there's an emergency and I can't get a hold of you?"

"Well, your friends have phones, right? You can borrow one of theirs."

"You're proving my point," I'd attempt to argue. "All my friends have phones. I need one too!" But my parents would not budge. I had to get creative with my communication to Myles, so I would text him from my mom's phone. This meant she could see everything we said, and I hated it.

Then, one day, Myles invited me to go to the movies with him. I asked my mom for permission, and she said, "I guess that would be okay, but I'm going with you." What?! I was disappointed but knew there was no way around it, so Mom tagged along with Myles' little sister in tow. We bought our tickets to see *New in Town*, a romantic comedy starring Renée Zellweger, and I bought a package of Sour Patch Kids. Myles and I made our way to a couple of seats in the center of the theater, and my mom and Myles' sister found their seats . . . in the row directly behind ours.

At one point in the movie, Myles extended his hand toward me with his palm facing up. I placed a Sour Patch Kid in his hand assuming he wanted one. He looked down at the piece of candy and then back up at me with confusion. Then he said, "Umm, no. I was trying to hold your hand." Now mortified, I quickly popped the Sour Patch Kid into my mouth and placed my hand in his. I tried to focus on the movie, but it was hopeless. I was holding hands with a guy, and it was the biggest deal ever! All the while, my mom's ever-present, protective eyes were witnessing it.

Myles and I "dated" for about three months, but we never really talked or hung out. We never kissed. He once texted me saying, "We don't act like boyfriend and girlfriend."

I typed back, "I don't know how to be a girlfriend. I've never done this before."

"Well, it's weird," he wrote back.

"OK," I answered, not knowing what else to say.

Then, after school one day, I was hanging outside with friends before play practice for *Beauty and the Beast*, the spring musical. I had been cast as one of three "silly girls." If you've seen the movie or the play, the silly girls are a trio who wear matching dresses in different colors. They fawn over Gaston and say, "He's dreamy!" This was an exciting role for me because it wasn't just an ensemble role.

Myles came up to me and asked to talk. As we walked away from my friends, he said, "Okay, I still really want to be friends, but I think we should break up."

My heart sank, but I was determined to put on a brave face and not let him see me cry. "Okay," I said. "Well, thanks for telling me how you feel."

He turned and walked away, and it immediately started to rain. And in typical, dramatic Betty fashion, I pictured myself right in the middle of a movie scene. I put my hands over my face and cried my eyes out while the rain drenched me from head to toe. I stood there thinking, *It's over. It's really over.* The dark sky perfectly matched the sadness I felt, and my tears blended in with the rain pouring down my face. It was my first breakup, and I was heartbroken.

Unfortunately, I still had to go to play practice, and I was not going to let this affect my acting. I went out onto the stage for my scene determined to give it all I had even though everyone could clearly see I had been crying. After practice, the director stopped me before leaving and asked, "Hey Betty, are you okay?" I told him Myles had broken up with me. He was apologetic and understanding. Then he said, "I'm really impressed you were able to put that experience aside and dedicate yourself to your character. You could have dragged your feelings out onto stage. I'm proud of your maturity, and you should be too." In all honesty, I was.

No one's first breakup is easy, even if it's only *kind of* a relationship, and mine was no exception. But I got through it. And as opening night approached, Eric, the guy who was cast as Gaston, caught my eye. We had a fleeting "showmance"—a silly, mutual theater crush—that helped lift my spirits after the breakup with Myles and helped me realize there were other guys in the world. As much as I liked Eric, he was two years older than me, so I chalked our relationship up as nothing more than a quick crush that would end as soon as the production was over.

After the final curtain call for *Beauty and the Beast*, I couldn't wait for my sophomore year and the fall play. I loved acting. Period. And the musicals were my favorite since they gave me a chance to sing and act. I knew once I was a sophomore, I would have a better chance at landing a lead role or at least a more important role. I couldn't wait to find out what our next show would be.

I entered my sophomore year and, of course, auditioned for the one-act play that fall, *Godspell*. Mikey was very talented at musical theater as well and participated in the shows at our school. That year, he landed the main role of Jesus in *Godspell*, and a guy in Mikey's class named Jake landed the role of Judas. This was another primarily ensemble show, and again I was cast in the ensemble. During practices, I started to notice that Jake was showing me a lot of attention but in that confusing, boyish way where they tease you because they actually like you.

Our family bonfire that year would give me the perfect opportunity to gauge Jake's potential interest in me. Every November, our family hosted a big bonfire at the farm. It was meant to coincide with Sophia's birthday, and hundreds of people would often come, usually friends, family, and employees from the Cantrell Center. I invited all my friends to the bonfire, and I made sure to include Jake, my new crush. I don't think it was a secret that we liked each other, and my friends were hounding me beforehand, asking me if I was going to kiss him.

"No, I am not kissing Jake," I asserted. I had never kissed anyone, but most of my friends had. Still, I was curious: "How do you do it?" I asked. "Like . . . what exactly do you do?"

"Oh, it's easy," they said. "You'll know what to do when it happens." Their response was totally useless. Even though I wasn't going to kiss Jake, their answer did nothing to calm my nerves. I knew I wasn't going to try to kiss him, but what if he tried to kiss me? What was I supposed to do? I was a nervous wreck.

The bonfire took place in our pecan orchard, which lined the part of the driveway closest to our house. My dad and Mikey would get the bonfire going by using broken limbs from the surrounding pecan trees, and people would walk back and forth between the party at the barn and the bonfire in the orchard with the moon to light their way. Most people hung out near the barn where there was food, drinks, and a band or karaoke.

At one point in the evening, Jake and I wandered away from the bonfire and stood behind a nearby pecan tree. We naturally leaned in at the same time for my very first kiss. It was really sweet. And my friends were right; it wasn't weird or awkward like I had feared, and when it happened, I knew what to do.

Still, the next day, I felt a little unnerved for having had my first kiss at fifteen. It felt too young—too early. As silly as it may sound, this kiss was a big deal to me. My friends had already had their first kisses, but for whatever reason, sixteen seemed a more appropriate age to me. Confused, I went to my parents and told them how I was feeling.

"I really wanted to wait until I was sixteen to have my first kiss," I said.

"Betty, it's okay. You are a teenager. This is normal and natural," they said. "Don't be so hard on yourself." They were more concerned about who I was kissing and when they'd get to meet him.

Jake broke up with me a month later at the senior baccalaureate mass right before Christmas break. He said he had too much on his mind as he prepared for college, and he didn't want to be dating anyone right now. Of course, I understood, but I was upset. I felt cool to be dating a senior, and this breakup proved tougher than the last.

Spring came, and I auditioned for the musical *Once on This Island.* Much to my surprise, I was given the lead female role—my very first one! It was a huge deal to me because the director rarely chose underclassmen for these kinds of challenging and demanding roles. I was thrilled, but I could tell some of the older girls in the production resented me for it. I felt their eyes fall on me as we scanned the cast list posted outside the director's office. They thought I was too young and that the role should have gone to a junior or a senior.

I couldn't blame them for being upset, so I tried not to show my excitement.

In the musical, my character, a peasant girl named Ti Moune, falls in love with a rich heir named Daniel Beauxhomme. And who would play Daniel in our production? None other than Eric, my crush from *Beauty and the Beast*! I still had a huge crush on him, and that made rehearsals way more exciting. We started spending more and more time together both before and after rehearsals, and I started to think maybe our feelings were more than just a showmance.

The problem was that Eric had a girlfriend. He kept telling me he was going to break up with her and be with me, but the longer I waited, the harder it became. I wasn't comfortable flirting with this guy who I knew was dating someone else. I was young and didn't know any better, so I waited and waited. Eric would tell me he loved me and wanted to be with me, but he never broke up with his girlfriend. The school year came to a close, and since I didn't have a phone, I had no way of keeping in touch with him when he went off to college. And then that was it. He moved on, and I had to as well. It was really hard, and my entire summer had an underlying sadness to it.

But there were bright spots to my summer too. I got my braces off, started to wear makeup, and learned how to fix my hair a bit. I felt more confident about my appearance, and all of these changes had me excited to start my junior year of high school. My parents obviously noticed the changes in me as well. I had a larger chest compared to many of my friends, and my middle-school awkwardness was now gone. My mom, probably knowing what laid ahead of me when I returned to school, shared her own high school experience with me. She told me how she had been thin and flat-chested until her sophomore year of high school. Then she blossomed and grew into herself, and when she went back to school, she told me about the unexpected attention she received and how overwhelming it felt.

When I went back to school my junior year, I was a whole new woman. But, just like my mom, I was completely unprepared for the attention I started to receive from boys. It was intoxicating in some ways—especially since I had felt like an awkward, heartbroken loser just the year before. I still didn't know how to be cool, and I only had a few friends who I liked to hang out with. But the attention from boys began to cause trouble, and people started to spread hurtful rumors about me. My parents had taught us that there would always be bullies, and the best way to handle them was to ignore them. They also taught us to stand up for ourselves whenever we felt we needed to. I chose to ignore the rumors and the girls spreading them, which was much easier said than done.

Even though I didn't know how to handle the attention from boys, I was not about to let it affect my morals. Most of my friends were sexually active, but I wanted to save myself for my future husband. This was of huge importance to me, and fortunately, I had the wisdom to understand that most high school boys—even those with the best of intentions—have sex on the brain. They're just wired that way. Guys would express their interest in dating me, but as soon as they realized I was serious about saving myself for marriage, they'd disappear. Had I not understood this about boys, I think it's very possible I could have given in to the pressure, and I know that's something I would have deeply regretted.

Before I knew it, my sixteenth birthday had rolled around. Shortly before that, my family watched an episode of *The Andy Griffith Show* where Aunt Bee is concerned that Opie, the sheriff's son, had been spending too much time at the jail. She says, "Well I wouldn't be surprised if at Opie's next birthday party, he shoots out the candles!" Of course, my family thought this was hilarious and decided this was a great idea for me to try at my party. My mom bought long-stemmed candles like the ones we used at church, and we pushed sixteen of them down into my birthday cake. We set the cake on a table on one side of the barn, and I took a seat at a table on the other side. I steadied myself, took careful aim, and shot every single candle!

My friends, who were all from the city, were impressed with and probably even a little shocked at my shooting skills. This was not something that took place at their parties.

Even though I could invite as many friends as I wanted to my birthday parties, I was never allowed to attend my friends' parties— even in high school, and mostly because their parties weren't nearly as tame as mine. They were more like actual parties, complete with music, dancing, drinking, and kids from the entire school, whereas mine included a barn, a cake, girlfriends, and a dove shoot. Well, I guess that's not entirely true. I was *allowed* to go to their parties, but only if my mom or dad went with me. Whenever I'd ask to attend one, my parents would give the same stipulation: "Sure. As long as we can go too."

"Never!" I'd shout. My parents at a party? Way too embarrassing.

My gift for my sixteenth birthday was my dream truck: a black, four-door Ford F-150. Only, I couldn't drive it because I didn't have my license yet. And I didn't have my license yet because my parents said I had to improve my grades first. It wasn't that they expected straight As, and I never had Ds or Fs on my report card. They just wanted to see fewer Bs and Cs. But I couldn't cut it. So, the truck sat in our yard for two years until my parents relented and let me get my license—*after* I graduated from high school.

As my voice lessons and play practices began taking up more and more of my time, I decided to quit ballet my junior year of high school. I had finally found my thing and my passion in music and acting. I loved theater, and I excelled at it. I landed lead roles that year in both the one-act play, *A Piece of My Heart,* in which I played Martha, and the spring musical, *Little Women,* in which I played Jo. In fact, when my school took *A Piece of My Heart* to a one-act competition in our region and later to our state competition, I won the "Best Actress" award.

Once my senior year rolled around, I began gaining notoriety among the local schools as a talented singer and actress. Singing and acting were becoming what I was known for, and people started to respect me for the work I put into performing. For the fall one-act play, *Dark of the Moon,* I got the lead role of Barbara Allen and won best actress again. Then for the spring musical, I played Dorothy in *The Wizard of Oz.* I loved embodying every nuance of Judy Garland and bringing that classic role to life. It was the perfect way to end my high school drama career.

Also, early in my senior year—and after years of begging my parents—I was finally allowed to have a cell phone. Everyone at the time was getting the first iPhone, but I insisted on being different. I had decided that iPhones were too mainstream, so my best friend from school, Savanna, and I got Blackberry Torches. We thought we were so cool, and this long-awaited freedom opened up a whole new world for me. I suddenly had this new way of keeping in touch with my friends. I could call and text them without using my mom's phone, and I loved it!

But every night before bed, I had to turn my phone in to my parents. They said it was to keep me from staying up all night, but they also used that time to read through my texts. If they found something they didn't like or approve of, I would lose phone privileges. I considered this a serious invasion of privacy and incredibly unfair. But now I see things a little differently. Looking back, sure, my parents made my life miserable as a teenager, but they also made me successful as an adult.

With my phone also came access to Facebook, and it didn't take long for me to experience cyberbullying. A few girls in my class and a couple girls who were older than me started sending me private messages. They'd call me awful names and make outrageous, inappropriate claims, like I had slept with the entire football team. Then they started to spread rumors. I genuinely didn't understand why this was happening. I hadn't done anything to these girls, yet it seemed like they were out to get me.

Given the things they were saying, I knew the bullying needed to be reported. I shared what I was experiencing with a trusted teacher, and she let me know that because of the nature and content of the messages they were sending me, Mount de Sales could prevent them from graduating. I thought about it and decided not to push it further. I figured if they didn't graduate, their senseless vendetta against me would only grow. This was a time to be the bigger person and forgive.

Some of my proudest moments from high school took place my senior year. A teacher nominated me to represent our school at a literary competition where I competed against other schools in the region across several disciplines, including math, art, and science to name just a few. I entered the singing category and won first place! Another teacher nominated me to represent our school at the Golden Eagle competition, which is reserved for high school students and includes twelve different disciplines. The awards are a golden eagle trophy and scholarship money. I competed in the music discipline, which is for singers and instrumentalists, and I won the Golden Eagle award for music. Winning these kinds of competitions helped validate my belief that my dreams were realistic. I could do it!

My commitment to singing and acting during my senior year took away what little focus I had left for my other studies. All I cared about was singing and acting. It was what I loved, and I knew it was what I wanted to do professionally. I wanted to skip high school and move on to college where I could finally focus on what I loved and not have to worry about algebra, physics, or any other subjects I dreaded.

As graduation approached, I began to get anxious. I was scared to leave my safe, comfortable life where I knew everyone and understood exactly where I fit. Even though I was nervous to go to college and make new friends, I also understood that change was an inevitable part of life. I had earned a voice and acting scholarship to Wesleyan, the same school where I took voice lessons, so I knew where I would be going in the literal sense. I knew I wanted to be a singer and an actress, and I knew I had what it took. What I didn't know was how I would turn that passion into a reality. It was an ambitious dream, and I was aware the statistics were not in my favor. But that was no reason to keep me from trying. I'm a strong believer that our fears and anxieties shouldn't stop us but should push us forward.

I started high school unsure of everything, and yet it all somehow seemed so important—every word, every test, every friend, every boy. Now I know that so little of that matters in the grand scheme of things. High school is such a small part of your life, even though it often feels like it can and will define you. The reality is that you will forget most of the people you knew in high school. It won't matter what someone may have said about you once upon a time.

What matters is that you figure out who you are and what you love to do and that you allow yourself to bloom. And this was true for me. I had walked into my first day of high school alone and uncertain, but I discovered my passion and purpose.

I began dreaming of what a future would look like beyond high school, and I started investing in those dreams one voice lesson, one play, and one musical at a time. And my hard work paid off. By the time I left school, I knew what my next step would be. I didn't have all the answers, and my path wouldn't be perfectly clear. There would be some twists and turns along the way. But I had my long-term goal in mind, and I was determined, with the help of my family and God, to make my dreams come true.

CHAPTER 5

Born to Perform

When the time came to apply for college, I submitted applications to two schools: Wesleyan College, where I had been taking my voice lessons, and the American Music and Dramatic Academy in Hollywood, California, which required an extensive audition process. Famous actors and singers like Jason Mraz, Jesse Tyler Ferguson, Janelle Monaé, and Caissie Levy had graduated from AMDA, and I couldn't believe it when I received an acceptance letter! I was offered a small scholarship, but it wasn't nearly enough to offset the enormous cost of moving *and* tuition. It was out of the question, but I was honored to have been accepted at all.

Wesleyan College, however, offered me a generous scholarship that was practically enough for a free education, and I wasn't passing that up. Wesleyan is a small, women's liberal arts school in Macon, Georgia. The campus is gorgeous, complete with historic, red-brick buildings and tall, white columns. In many ways, the campus already felt like home to me since I had been taking voice lessons there for several years. I also admired Wesleyan's rich historical background and looked forward to being part of it. It was the first college in the world chartered to grant degrees to women, and I loved its dedication to women's education. But I was also nervous about going to an all-girls school and unsure as to whether or not I would like it.

Since Macon is only a forty-minute drive from Fort Valley, I didn't live on campus. It made sense to commute from home and save money instead. I was pumped for my first day of college. My entire high school experience, for me anyway, was all about appearances and social interactions, and I had always been limited to a uniform. Excited to express my personal style, I spent the entire night beforehand carefully planning my outfit.

I couldn't wait to drive my F-150 to campus that morning. I drove all the way down our three-mile dirt driveway, and just when I pulled out onto the two-lane highway, my rear left tire blew out! At first, I thought it was just a flat tire, but when I climbed out to check, the rubber was shredded from a huge nail lodged inside of it. I was going to be late on my very first day of school. Crying my eyes out, I called my dad. He left work to pick me up and drive me to Macon for my first day. I was late and so embarrassed when I had to walk into the introduction assembly with all the other freshmen already sitting in their seats. I did my best to slink into a seat undetected, and I don't think I processed a single word from that assembly. I was too busy trying to recover from the embarrassment.

My major was theatre, and I was minoring in music. Ideally, I would have majored in musical theatre, but few schools offer that degree, especially in Georgia. Like most freshmen, most of my classes were core, general education classes, which I did not enjoy. They were tough. And my schedule only permitted me to enroll in one theatre class, but I was so anxious to focus on my major and get away from learning the same stuff I had learned in high school. I didn't like math or history then, and I wasn't about to change my mind.

Within the first couple of months, I realized Wesleyan wasn't a good fit for me. Making friends was still a challenge, and most days, I would drive to campus, attend my classes, and immediately come home. I felt like I was missing out on the traditional college experience by not attending a school with both guys and girls. I felt depressed, and I just wasn't enjoying the college experience like many of my friends at other universities were. So, toward the end of my freshman year, I decided to transfer to Mercer University—also in Macon—for my second year. My boyfriend at the time, Mick, was less than thrilled about my decision.

Mick and I had met during our senior year of high school at a thespian conference for theater students. He was super cute by any girl's standards. He had a nice face, nice hair, *and* he enjoyed theatre! I also liked that he was serious about our relationship. He was living in Atlanta with his family, but he would drive down to see me, or I would drive up to see him a lot. Our moms were always in close communication to make sure I arrived safely, and if I spent the night, they made sure Mick and I slept in separate bedrooms.

After that summer ended and we both started college, we saw each other less. He was studying accounting at Georgia Southern University, which was about two and a half hours south of Macon, so we had a long-distance relationship. Between classes and the commute, it was hard to find time to see each other. He would sometimes drive up on the weekends and spend the weekend with me at my parents' house, but I wasn't allowed to visit him at GSU since there wasn't supervision.

When I first told Mick I was transferring to Mercer, he was nervous. It had never occurred to me beforehand that he probably liked me attending an all-girls school. I imagine it gave him peace of mind to know I wasn't surrounded by stereotypical frat boys all day. In fact, Mick's greatest fear in terms of our relationship was that I'd meet someone else at Mercer. He didn't like that I was transferring, but it was my decision. It was going to happen regardless.

Also, toward the end of my freshman year, my mom started talking to me about the Miss America Organization. A member at the Cantrell Center was the local director of the Miss Warner Robins Pageant, and she told my mom all about it and suggested I consider competing. At first, I totally blew off the idea. I had zero interest in pageants, and I certainly wasn't going to be a pageant girl. I fully believed the stereotype that pageant girls were catty, superficial mean girls with big hair, and I wanted no part in it.

But when my mom brought it up again, she mentioned the scholarship money and the talent portion of the competition. If I competed and won a local title, I could compete at Miss Georgia and win scholarship money to pay for school *and* potentially launch my music career. That seemed like a win-win to me. I decided it couldn't hurt to try one pageant, and, who knew, maybe I'd even like it. I researched the Miss Warner Robins Pageant, which was to take place that summer before my sophomore year.

I had zero experience with pageants, and I had no idea what I had gotten myself into. I could not have been more clueless. I knew there were several categories within a pageant, including talent, evening gown, swimsuit, and an interview portion, but I had no idea how to prepare. I didn't realize that pageantry was its own world and many of the girls had been living in that world for years.

Before the Miss Warner Robins pageant, participants had to attend rehearsals to learn where and when to walk and stand during the pageant. All the girls showed up to that first rehearsal looking gorgeous and totally put together. They wore trendy Lily Pulitzer outfits, and their hair and nails were on point. I showed up in gym shorts, sneakers, and a T-shirt. I stuck out like a sore thumb. Not to mention all of the girls already knew each other from former pageants. They had their own community, so yet again, I had found myself in a situation where I knew no one. I felt like a total misfit.

Since I wasn't convinced pageants would be a long-term thing for me, I didn't spend a lot of money on my gown, clothing, makeup, or accessories. The other girls had stunning gowns from professional pageant designers like Sherri Hill, Jovani, and Mac Duggal. I decided to borrow a gown from my Aunt Dodie who had competed in the Miss America Organization in the seventies. It was an older dress, but it was hardly dated in terms of fashion. It was covered in black beading, and the neck was lined with transparent black mesh. Gold beading work accented the bust, and I thought it was gorgeous.

For the swimsuit portion of the pageant, I bought a two-piece black swimsuit from Victoria's Secret that also had gold trim to match my evening gown. I always thought their swimsuits were pretty and flattering, so it made sense to me. Again, I had missed the memo: the other girls' swimsuits were from pageant swimsuit sponsors like Kandice Pelletier and Jamye Shaw, and I didn't even know pageant swimsuit sponsors were a thing. To me, a swimsuit was a swimsuit, but it turned out that mine was the kind you swim in, and theirs were strictly made for walking on a stage. Naturally, their swimsuits looked and fit differently—much better than mine!

The talent portion of the competition was obviously the most important to me. Since contestants are only given ninety seconds to perform, I wanted to select a song that would showcase my voice. I ended up choosing "Astonishing" from *Little Women*, which is very hard to perform because the notes are long and high. But I'd sung it before when I played the character of Jo during the spring musical my junior year of high school, so I knew I could belt it out.

The pageant was held at the Warner Robins Civic Center. That morning, the board interviewed us, and the rest of the pageant would take place in the evening. To my interview, I wore red, fitted, high-waisted pants, a white camisole, which I tucked into my pants, and a cropped, striped suit jacket with nude heels. I later found out all the other girls wore dresses. Unsurprisingly, I didn't know how to do pageant hair and makeup. I just did what I thought would look pretty and hoped for the best.

My parents, Mick, friends, and employees from the Cantrell Center all attended the pageant that night to support me. I felt like I had nailed my talent, but I had no idea how I did in the other categories. As competitive as I am, I obviously wanted to win, but I knew the other girls had much more experience. My strategy was simply to do my best and try to mimic the other girls with the hope that I didn't look like a total misfit. I figured they would do much better than me anyway, so my attitude was to go into the whole experience without any expectations whatsoever.

Winners are announced for the talent and swimsuit preliminary events of the competition, and then there are also overall winners. When I was announced the winner of the talent portion, I was beyond excited! I cared more about my talent being recognized than winning the whole thing, and that was all the validation I needed. Then, when my name was announced as the first runner-up, I was shocked. My whole section of supporters erupted into loud cheers. They were hooting and hollering! I couldn't believe I snagged first runner-up, and the other girls in the pageant seemed equally surprised.

Even though I didn't win, I was proud of myself. I dared to step into a totally different world without any experience or training, and I gave it my best. I felt like I had done pretty well too considering it was my first time. And I was honestly surprised by how much fun I had. I truly enjoyed competing, so I started to think that maybe I should try this pageant thing again.

My sophomore year at Mercer began, and that September, I competed in the Miss Macon pageant. For this pageant, I invested in a nicer gown. It was still cheap compared to the other girls' gowns, but at least it was made within the present decade. I won swimsuit, but I didn't win talent. Overall, I placed as second runner-up. *Okay*, I thought. *I'll try one more time.*

The next pageant was Miss Capital City. I won talent and placed as first runner-up. At this point, I started to get frustrated. I was getting better and better, but I just couldn't seem to clinch the title. As I watched the winner be crowned, I decided internally it was time to give up pageants.

Then, Alicia Long, a field director for the Miss Georgia pageant who's basically in charge of the southeastern region of all Georgia local pageants, approached me after the competition and introduced herself. "Betty, I know you don't know me," she said. "I'm a field director for Miss Georgia. I want you to know you have such incredible potential, and you need to try one more pageant."

My frustration at losing again eased as I listened to her.

"It's in November in Americus, Georgia," she said. "It's the Miss Historic Southern Plains/Presidential Pathways Pageant, and I know you can win. They give out two titles, and you've been first runner-up almost every time you've competed."

I thanked Alicia and considered her suggestion. With her encouragement, I decided I would try one last time, so I made plans to compete for the Miss Presidential Pathways pageant.

Even though I continued to live at home while attending Mercer, I finally started to make friends. Mercer turned out to be an all-around better fit for me, and I was loving it! I had so much fun cheering on the Mercer Bears at their football games and singing with the Mercer Singers chorale group. My classes, on the other hand, were still hard for me. Very hard. I was struggling with music theory and the math of music, but I loved my voice lessons. I wished I could bypass the difficult classes and just sing and act!

Shortly into the school year, Mick called to tell me he was going to transfer to a school in Macon to be closer to me. I was confused. I cared about Mick and didn't want his dreams to change just because I was going to a new school with boys.

"But you want to go to the University of Georgia?" I said, confused. "You've talked about transferring to UGA, getting your accounting degree, and working for Ernst & Young. You have all these dreams. Why would you give it all up just so you can be closer to me?"

"It'll be fine," he assured me. "I'll get a job, and you can be a stay-at-home mom or a music teacher. You don't have to be a singer." He went on to explain how he could make enough money as an accountant, and then I wouldn't have to try to be famous. He was a practical person.

I seriously considered Mick's plans for us. After all, I deeply cared for him and wanted to be with him. We had been dating for a little over a year now, and I had started to see a future together. I had always dreamt of marriage, and I felt like Mick could maybe be "the one."

I decided to talk it through with my parents. "You know, I think I'm going to teach instead of try to become a singer," I told them. "Besides, Mick and I are going to get married, and it's a much more realistic plan."

"Are you sure that's what you want, Betty?" I could tell they weren't sold on the idea. "Why don't you give it some time and think about it more. Really consider what you're giving up." They later confessed to me that they were terrified. But at the time, they listened and supported me. I'm impressed by their patience and so grateful for their willingness to let me figure things out on my own.

The more I thought about Mick's plans for us, and the further I got into my sophomore year at Mercer, the more I realized I *didn't* want that life. Mick was championing what *he* wanted, and in doing so, he was not only jeopardizing my dream but also his own. That wasn't fair to either of us, and that was not how I wanted my life to go. We wanted different things, and I didn't want either of us to compromise what we wanted for ourselves just so we could be together.

The reality was that we needed to break up and go our separate ways. I knew that was the right thing to do, so I mustered the strength and courage to say the words. It was awful, and we were both heartbroken. The life we had imagined together suddenly disappeared. It would have been so much easier for me to stick with our plan and let both of us give up on our dreams. But I'm glad I didn't. Mick was my first real boyfriend, and the first person I had ever broken up with.

Looking back, I'm so grateful my first real relationship was with him because he genuinely cared about me. He was very sweet and an all-around good guy; he just wasn't the right guy for me.

After my breakup with Mick, I began dating Edgar, a guy I had met at the beginning of the school year. Edgar was two years ahead of me in school and a double major in biology and music, but he was not your typical music student. Most music students are intensely serious, prefer to keep to themselves, and only want to talk about music. Edgar was different; he was a total bro. He raced bicycles competitively and played darts at a bar every Wednesday. I liked that he didn't take himself too seriously. Instead, he was super funny, laid-back, and effortlessly cool, and he helped distract me from the pain of my breakup with Mick.

The whole time we were together, though, Edgar was very close with his ex. He had broken up with her to date me, so their breakup was fresh. But he continued to text and talk to her on the phone—a *lot*. It bothered me, of course, and every time I tried to talk to him about it, he'd say, "Well, she was my best friend before we started dating, so we're just best friends again."

Edgar was only my second serious boyfriend, and his reasoning made enough sense to me to ignore their friendship. For whatever reason, it didn't register as a red flag, so I tried not to make it a big deal. I honestly didn't know whether my concern was justified or not, and I totally lacked the confidence to confront him about it any further. I also thought I might be in the wrong to pressure him about it. Still, it felt unfair to me and made me feel like I wasn't good enough.

My focus shifted to pageants, and in November, I won my first title in the Miss Georgia system as Miss Presidential Pathways! Alicia was right after all—I could win! But what I had completely forgotten was that a local title win means you are *required* to compete at the Miss Georgia pageant in June. Of course, I had been hoping to get to Miss Georgia, but in no way was I ready for a pageant on that level just yet. I'd only competed in four pageants, whereas most girls had been competing for years. Luckily, the board of directors for Miss Presidential Pathways mentors their winner and helps her prepare for Miss Georgia, and I was definitely going to need their help.

Unless you've been in pageants, you wouldn't believe just how much preparation goes into them. The board of directors helped me pick out a real evening gown, a real swimsuit, and a real pageant wardrobe. I attended hair and makeup lessons. I had professional head shots taken by pageant photographers. I was working with a personal trainer every day in preparation for the swimsuit competition, and I was practicing my talent and doing mock interviews. The interview portion requires contestants to have a ten-minute, private interview with judges in which they ask you about your résumé, platform, politics, and current events. I was studying my butt off!

On the board of directors was a woman named Linda, and she was in charge of helping me prepare for Miss Georgia. She is a sweet woman who I love to this day. Shortly after I won Miss Presidential Pathways, Linda introduced me over the phone to her sister Hester. Hester told me of the potential I had and how she thought I had a really good chance at becoming Miss Georgia. She offered to help me prepare, and I agreed wholeheartedly. I was thrilled and relieved to have someone help me get ready for the competition. "We're going to get you ready for Miss Georgia," she said. "It's going to be tough, but you're going to win." Even though Hester wasn't on the board of directors, from then on, she became my main point of communication, and I hardly communicated with Linda or anyone else on the board.

Hester prepared daily schedules for me—every single day. She would email detailed, minute-by-minute instructions: "Wake up at 7:30. By 7:35, you should be done brushing your teeth and starting on your sit-ups. Do one hundred sit-ups before 8:00. By 8:00, you should be eating breakfast. Finish breakfast by 8:20 and begin writing a paper for me. Turn your paper into me by 5:00 p.m." She would give me a list of books to read, and then I would have to write papers on them for her to review. It was like school, and I absolutely hated it.

Hester is demanding of me, I thought. *If this helps me win, it will be worth it.* Like my parents and my former ballet teacher, I responded well to strong leadership. Besides, I had no idea what pageant coaching looked like. I had no other coaches or experiences to compare Hester to.

As I continued to prepare, however, I was fortunate to work with other mentors. Thomas Barnett helped me select my talent piece. During our first session together, he asked me if I knew what I wanted to sing. I told him I was conflicted: "I sing all genres, but I feel like I should choose a Broadway piece or a classical opera aria."

His expression told me he was skeptical. "Are you even classically trained?" he asked.

"Yep. I've been taking classical voice lessons since age fourteen."

"Alright," he said, "sing a little opera for me."

I started singing a German piece I had worked on with my vocal coach. About fifteen seconds into the piece, he stopped me.

"Wow! You don't need to be singing anything but opera." He complimented my skill and range. "I've only given this special piece to one other pageant girl, but she never got the chance to perform it on the Miss America stage. I believe you could be the one to do it."

Then he introduced me to "Tu, Tu, Piccolo Iddio" from *Madame Butterfly*, and I immediately fell in love with the song. It was so powerful and dramatic that it sent chills up my spine. I couldn't wait to perform it.

Thomas also taught me how to walk. He was an amazing coach, and he's famous in the pageant industry for having worked with many Miss Americas and Miss USAs. He's a dear friend of mine to this day, and I'm so blessed to have had the opportunity to work with him.

Then there was Chuck Fallis, another fantastic coach I worked with. He helped me prepare for my interview, and he was just the sweetest. We'd meet at Starbucks, and he always brought newspaper clippings he had cut out. He'd hand them to me and say, "Here's what's happening in the news. What's your opinion on this? What side do you fall on?" I'd tell him, and then he'd say, "Okay, here's how to word that correctly in your interview."

So many coaches tend to pressure their contestants into parroting whatever they believe. But Chuck never told me how to think or what to say. He respected my personal opinions and helped me craft articulate, informed responses. He wanted *me* to shine through—not his own political agenda. I hugely appreciated that, and I still keep in touch with him too.

I continued to prepare for Miss Georgia, but I took a short break over Valentine's Day weekend with Edgar to visit his family in Atlanta. While there, my dad called me. This wasn't unusual, but I immediately sensed his tone was strange.

"Betty, you need to come home." He was serious.

"What? Why?"

"You need to come home now," he practically ordered.

"What's going on?" I asked. Now I was concerned. I started to think I was in trouble, but I wasn't sure what I'd done.

"Just get home as soon as you can."

I drove all the way home from Atlanta, a two-and-a-half-hour drive, with my stomach in knots. I walked into the house and saw Mikey, Sophia, and my parents sitting in in a circle in the living room.

"What is going on?" I asked. It had been a long drive, and this question had played on repeat in my head the entire time. I took a seat between Mikey and Sophia.

My dad started to stammer. I could tell he was searching for the right words. He gave up and bluntly said, "Your mother and I are getting a divorce."

Mikey, Sophia, and I were completely caught off guard. We never suspected a thing. In our eyes, we were the ultimate family who everyone loved and wanted to be a part of. We were the Von Trapp Family Singers for crying out loud. After a long, awkward, emotional conversation among the five of us, I needed to be alone. I needed privacy to let all of my emotions out. I got into my truck and left without a destination in mind. I cried hard and even screamed. I was sad, angry, and confused.

My parents' divorce had totally rocked our world, and we all dealt with it in our own ways. Mikey was finishing up his senior year at the University of Georgia, so he wasn't home much. I was focused on school and pageants, which kept me busy and definitely helped keep my mind off of my parents. But Sophia took the brunt of it. She was only fourteen and still at home.

Once June finally rolled around, it was time for Miss Georgia. Again, I was in a situation where I didn't know anybody. I wanted to make friends, but people have told me that when I'm in competition mode, I become unusually quiet and keep to myself. It's not something I consciously do; I just get hyper-focused and totally live inside my own head. I've since realized this can come across as rude, intimidating, or unfriendly—none of which makes it easy to make friends. It also didn't help that I was new and doing fairly well, and I think this made some of the more seasoned girls a little nervous. Like any other kind of competitive sport or activity, people are wary of the new person with potential.

The Miss Georgia Pageant consists of three nights of preliminary events which lead up to the final night. The first night of the preliminaries arrived, and Edgar let me know beforehand that he wouldn't be able to come to any of them. I was a little disappointed he wouldn't be there to root for me, but I understood he had other things to do, and he promised to come to the final night. Besides, it was a long drive for him, and the pageant livestreams the preliminary nights online, so he could watch them from home.

After the first prelim night, I was feeling excited and called Edgar: "So what did you think? I think I did pretty good, right?"

"What are you talking about," he said. "How would I know?"

"You didn't watch the livestream?" I asked, hurt. I had told him about it days ago.

"No, tonight was dart night." He was so nonchalant about it, and his lack of interest upset me.

"Are you serious? You know how big of a deal this is, and you didn't even watch me?"

"It's just the prelim nights. I didn't know."

Whatever, I thought. I was tired, and I still had a few days left of the competition. It wasn't worth wasting my energy.

The final night came, and Edgar sat in the audience with my family. I won the preliminary and overall talent awards and placed second runner-up out of forty contestants, most of whom were experienced pageant girls. I was over the moon with excitement, and my family was beyond proud.

Wow, I thought. *Maybe I could actually clinch this thing next year!* I knew I had to try again. If I won Miss Georgia, I could compete in Miss America. And if I made it far enough in the Miss America competition, I could sing on national television. If I could sing on national television, I could get my voice out there for somebody to hear, and maybe someone would want to sign me for a record deal. It was a long shot, for sure, but it wasn't impossible.

With dreams of my potential future filling my head, I changed out of my gown and into regular clothes to meet up with my family and Edgar. We were all excited from the night's events, so we went out to eat together. After dinner, Edgar said he was going to head home. I was surprised. We were in Columbus, Georgia, which was a three-hour drive from his home in Atlanta, and it was almost eleven o'clock at night.

"I haven't seen you in like two weeks. You don't want to hang out for a bit?"

"I really want to make it to the race tomorrow," he said. "Besides, it's not like you won or anything."

As he drove back to Atlanta, I decided I was done with Edgar. I didn't feel like a priority to him, and I was uncomfortable with the closeness he and his ex-girlfriend shared from day one of our relationship. We had been dating for nine months and discussed a future together, but I had had it. I'm not good with confrontation, so needless to say, it didn't go well. I added another messy breakup to my list and swore to myself that the next guy I dated would be someone who cared about me and supported my dreams. But I needed a break from serious relationships. I wanted to try dating in a more casual sense to figure out what I wanted and what I didn't want.

At that point, my friends told me about a dating app, and it took some convincing on their part for me to create an account. I was a full-time student working at an interior design and home décor boutique in Perry, Georgia, on the weekends *and* preparing for pageants, so it's not like I had spare time to go out and meet people organically. I created a profile, started swiping, and then went on a flurry of dates. They were all perfectly nice guys, but I knew immediately that they weren't for me. Some of them looked completely unlike their profile pictures, some were attractive but lacked intellectual qualities, and some were just looking for hookups—not my style. I was too busy for these kinds of dates, so I let my dating life fall to the wayside.

My second chance at Miss Georgia began with the Miss Warner Robins pageant in July 2014—just before my junior year of college. I brought my A game to this pageant because I was so excited to be competing again for my hometown title, and I really wanted to take it to Miss Georgia. I didn't sing my Italian aria because I wanted to save it for Miss Georgia, so I performed "So Small" by Carrie Underwood. I won talent and swimsuit, and then I was crowned Miss Warner Robins 2015! The grueling prep for Miss Georgia started up once again, which meant Hester had me back on her rigid daily schedules and was closely clocking my time.

Summer ended, and on my first day of my junior year at Mercer, I met Rex. That morning, I had put extra effort into looking nice since it was the first day of classes. I had done my makeup and was wearing a flowy, floral dress. While walking on campus, I passed this seriously attractive, James Franco lookalike. We exchanged smiles, and he winked at me!

My year is off to a good start, I thought, but I didn't really think more of it. I had no way of knowing who he was. Not only did I not know his name, but I was also fairly isolated in the music school. All of my classes were in that building, so I rarely met anyone outside of it.

One of my friends in the music school told me about a date she was going on after class that evening, and she asked me to drop her off at his place. He lived very close to Mercer, so I was happy to give her a ride. When we arrived at his apartment, she said, "Come up with me and meet him." I thought that was a little strange, but I agreed. She knocked on the door, and when I saw the guy who opened it, I thought, *Whoa!* I'd seen him before. It was the same guy who had winked at me earlier that morning.

"Betty, this is Rex," my friend said.

I could tell he recognized me too, so I introduced myself: "Hi, nice to meet you. I'm Betty. Well, you two have fun on your date!" I said and quickly left.

Later that night, Rex sent me a Facebook message: "Hey, Betty. So my date is over."

"Oh, how did it go?" I replied. It seemed polite to ask—even though I had a pretty good idea of where this conversation was going. He said it went fine, but there wouldn't be a second date. Then he asked if I wanted to hang out.

Rex and I started hanging out, but we were not seeing each other exclusively. He never wanted to take me out on dates, and we only spent time together when it was convenient for him. Even then, it was always, "Hey, come over to my apartment," and never, "Let me take you out to dinner." I held on to a foolish hope that we might develop a committed relationship. He strung me along for months and months before I finally admitted to myself that I was only putting up with his noncommittal attitude because he was a good-looking mystery man and fun to be around. I was being shallow.

Just as I was growing tired of Rex's indecision, Edgar came back into my life. He had already graduated, but since it was the beginning of the school year, he was back on campus for the homecoming football game. I saw him there, and he asked if we could talk. I hadn't seen him for months, and at first it was awkward. But then I suddenly remembered why I liked him so much: he's fun and easy to be around. Edgar was familiar and comfortable.

I broke things off with Rex, and Edgar and I got back together. About a week later, though, I asked myself, *What am I doing? This didn't work out the first time; why did I think it would work the second?* I had fallen right back into the same pattern of compromising what I wanted, so I broke up with Edgar—again. I called Rex: "Look, Rex, I like you. I shouldn't have gone back to Edgar." But it was too late according to Rex. He was upset that I had chosen Edgar over him.

Frustrated at my failing dating life and how much of a mess I was making with relationships, not to mention my home life was a wreck with my parents' looming divorce, I threw myself into preparations for Miss Georgia harder than ever. I was giving it just about everything I had—so much so that the dean of Mercer's music school noticed and called me into his office.

"Betty, we're worried about your grades, and you're not performing very well in your classes," he said. "We think you need to focus more on school and less on pageants."

He was right. While I loved my voice lessons, I hated my classes, and it showed in my grades. I'm a smart girl, but my brain does not understand music theory. No matter how hard I tried, it never seemed to click. But the dean was also wrong. He couldn't see what I saw. I wasn't doing pageants for the sake of winning pageants; I saw pageants as a pathway to my dream. I am genuinely grateful for the dean for having cared enough to express his concern, but I had to trust my gut on this one.

My ambition tends to give me tunnel vision—for better or for worse—so I made the tough decision to take the second semester of my junior year off to focus completely on Miss Georgia. It wasn't an easy decision, and I fully recognized the risks I was taking, but I also knew I stood a much better chance of achieving my dreams through the Miss America Organization than I did with a music degree. I also ran the idea by my parents and Hester, and they were all supportive. They agreed Miss America could be an enormous stepping stone to becoming a singer/actress.

My time in college taught me a lot about myself. I learned if an environment or a community isn't right for you, then you can take the initiative and find one that is. Wesleyan may not have been a great fit for me, but I blossomed at Mercer. I learned not to compromise my dreams for a romantic relationship and that I needed a partner who would make me a priority—someone who cherished me. I learned I had a resilience within me that I may have never found had I not gone through heartbreak. My parents' divorce taught me that life doesn't always turn out like you plan, and there is no such thing as a perfect family. Even the ones who appear perfect have their own issues and problems to work through.

The most exciting thing I learned from my two and a half years in college was that I was born to perform. I may not have been great at academics, music theory, or tests, and that was okay. Something inside me just couldn't shut off my desire to perform on a stage. I didn't let my shortcomings stop me; I just turned my attention toward what I *am* good at and gave it my all. I now had a vision of how I could use my talent and passion to fulfill my dream of becoming a singer and actress. And I was ready to put all my efforts into hitting it dead on.

CHAPTER 6

Meeting "the One" on the Way to Miss Georgia

was deep into Miss Georgia preparations in the fall of 2014, when one day, my mom approached me and said, "Betty, there's a group of guys visiting our church from Greece. You should take them out with your friends. Show them a good time in Macon." She loved the idea of me marrying a Greek guy, and her attempt at a setup was anything but subtle.

"Okay, Mom," I said. "This is literally the first time you've ever encouraged me to hang out with guys. I know what you're up to."

The guys hardly spoke English, and I knew this wasn't going anywhere, but I was able to convince a friend to join us at a club in downtown Macon. Clubs are not at all my scene. I've always been a homebody, so I was completely out of my element. Once there, the guys started mingling and looked like they were having fun. Meanwhile, I stood off to the side, awkward and visibly uncomfortable. When my friend left early, I envied her and wondered how much longer I would have to stick around before I could go home, change into pajamas, and watch a movie. Shortly after her departure, a young guy with a cane approached me and asked what I was doing standing alone.

"I'm just here with some people, but they sort of ditched me," I told him.

"Do you want to step outside and talk?"

"Sure," I said. I certainly didn't want to be in the club anymore, and lots of other people were standing outside. As we walked, I noticed he was limping.

He introduced himself as Brad. He was twenty-seven, and he was a veteran who spent time in Iraq. He had a shaved head and great bone structure. He lit a cigarette.

Gross, I thought. This guy was smoking, and he told me he was covered in tattoos. Not my type. But I appreciated how upfront and honest he was.

We continued small talk for a bit, and he asked for my number. I'm the type of girl who is too nice to say no sometimes, so I gave it to him. I would rather say yes and simply not text back than make it awkward in the moment. I was unsure of him, and the first time he texted me, I didn't text back right away. Instead, I looked him up on Facebook and saw he was legit. He had pictures of his time in Iraq and lots of military friends. I decided to give Brad a chance.

We started texting back and forth and hanging out, and I started to really like him. I was still living at home, and my protective parents couldn't help but treat me like a little kid, keeping close tabs on me at all times.

Brad and I were watching a movie at his apartment one day when I got a call from my mom.

"Where are you?" she asked.

"I'm hanging out with a guy."

"What guy?" She started grilling me with questions about him, and it was embarrassing, especially in front of Brad.

"Mom, please. I'm an adult," I said and ended the call.

Almost immediately, my dad called. My stomach tensed up. My parents were still going through their divorce, so if my mom and dad were in communication over this, I knew I was in trouble. Nervous, I answered the phone.

"Let me talk to this guy," my dad demanded.

"What? No!"

"I'm talking to him right now, Betty." I handed the phone to Brad and tried to disappear into the couch cushions.

I didn't know what my dad was saying to Brad, but Brad's responses were respectful: "Yes, sir. . . . No, sir, she's in good hands."

Brad handed the phone back to me, and my dad asked, "How long will it take you to get home?"

"Probably like thirty minutes."

"If you're not here in thirty minutes, I will come find you."

"Okay, okay." I jumped up, said goodbye to Brad, and got my butt home in record time!

Brad and I continued to see each other, but, like with Rex, we weren't dating exclusively. Whenever I shared my dreams of being Miss America and becoming a singer and actress, he'd say, "All of those are pipe dreams, Betty. What's your plan B?"

"Well, I guess my plan B is to become a music teacher or study early childhood education."

"Okay," he said. "Your plan B needs to be your plan A. You need to give up on all this stuff about becoming famous. It's dumb."

I had already been with someone who tried to deter me from my dreams, so I didn't let Brad's opinion faze me. But his criticisms became more frequent, and I felt like he was starting to belittle me. Then one day, I texted him to see if he wanted to hang out.

"I'm in Miami." He wrote back.

"Oh, when are you coming back?" I asked.

"I'm not coming back. I moved here."

What in the world?! I thought. I really, really liked this guy, and he moved without telling me? "Well, thanks for telling me," I texted back sarcastically.

"If you want to be with me so badly, I can just fly you down here," he said.

"I can't come to Miami." *Was he out of his mind?*

"You're an adult; you can make your own decisions. You should just move here. I can get you into realty school, and you can become a realtor."

"That's about the craziest thing I've ever heard in my life," I answered.

I talked to my mom about my conversation with Brad. She, of course, was not having any of it, but I entertained the idea for a minute: "Well, why not? It could be fun." In my head, I was trying to make sense of it all because I still liked Brad and wanted to be with him. After thinking about it and talking to my mom more, I thankfully realized just how insane the idea was. I had been here before but with Mick. Realty was not my passion; singing and acting were.

I told Brad I couldn't move to Miami, and he ended it. I was heartbroken. I thought I had found a mature guy who cared about me, but he ditched me. The fact that he was able to up and move without even telling me made me feel worthless, immature, and foolish. *What am I doing with my life?* I asked myself.

It was tough to get over Rex and then Brad back to back. It's all too easy to lose sight of what you truly want during the dating process. You find yourself compromising on things you ordinarily never would because a guy is handsome, or funny, or talented, or sweet. You ignore the signs he's not the one for you, and you get caught up in superficial things that don't matter.

Needless to say, I needed a break and deleted my dating app. I wanted to spend more time with my friends and focus on myself for a while. And I did. I took a hiatus from dating for a few months.

Eventually, I was ready to give it another try. Miss Georgia was only a few months away, and I didn't have much spare time, so I re-downloaded the app—again for its convenience. I prayed a lot: *God, please let me find the guy I'm supposed to be with. I'm sick of dating. I'm ready to find him. Please show him to me.*

The first profile that popped up on the app was for a guy named Spencer. He looked different in all of his photos but good in every single one, so I swiped right. He had a handsome face and a muscular body. His bio also said he was a graduate of The Citadel, the well-known military college in South Carolina. *Impressive*, I thought.

He messaged me and said, "Hi. I'm getting ready for work, but if you want to text me, I would love to talk to you."

My first impression was: *Okay, he's respectful, and he's got a job.* I wrote back, "Hi, I'm Betty, and yeah, I would love to talk to you. Let me know when you're off work."

"I can text a little at work," he wrote. "I'm a cop."

Because he looked so different in all of his pictures, I was feeling a little skeptical, so I asked if he'd send me a selfie, and he did. He was wearing his sheriff's deputy uniform, and he looked good—like shockingly good.

He wrote, "If you're comfortable exchanging numbers, I would love to text you. Here's my number." I already loved how respectful he was. I trusted him and gave him my number. We texted a bit that night, but he was busy at work, so we didn't get into any deep conversations.

A couple of days passed, and I'm not sure why, but we hadn't texted further. I just assumed Spencer wasn't interested, so I'd kind of forgotten about our messages. The next time I heard from him was when I was on a date with a guy who worked for my parents at the Cantrell Center. When my phone buzzed, I read Spencer's text: "Hey, remember me?" I suddenly *did* remember him, and I also remembered that I was really interested. I started texting him back. I didn't want to be completely rude to the guy I was having dinner with, so I wrapped up the date a little early. I couldn't help myself; I was too excited to text with Spencer.

I returned home, and we continued to text. At one point in our conversation, I said, "I want to hear what you sound like. Send me a voice text." Of course, I would have preferred a phone call, but in my experience, guys hated talking on the phone. They just want to text, and then to get them to actually hang out with you is a whole other ballgame.

Spencer proved to be much different from the other guys, though. He said, "A voice text? That's so weird, but okay." In the voice text he sent, he said, "I'm Spencer, and this is really weird." It made me laugh, and he had a nice voice—deep with a southern accent.

Then he said, "Why don't we just talk on the phone?"

"You're okay with that?" I asked. *Who was this guy?* He called me, and I was struck by how easy it felt to talk to him. We dove right into conversation, and it was like we had known each other forever. We had so much in common and tons of mutual friends since we had both attended private high schools in Macon. It was crazy that our paths hadn't crossed before. I had to meet him.

"So when are we going to hang out?" I asked. "I want to meet you in person."

"I don't have to work on Friday. How about then?"

"Okay, I can do Friday." We kept talking, and my interest in him only grew. I said, "I want to meet you sooner. What are you doing tomorrow?"

"Nothing," he answered.

"Well, let's hang out tomorrow."

"Okay. You can come over to my apartment."

I had to think about this. *His apartment? That seems a little too private.* My mom taught me to always meet a guy in a public place for the first time to be safe.

"That'll be fine," I said. Our conversation continued, and it was effortless. We already really liked each other. "What if when we see each other for the first time, it's like a movie, and we just have to kiss because it's perfect all in the moment?"

"You know what," Spencer said, "I think it's very likely that it could happen exactly like that."

We ended up talking for three hours that night, and before we ended our conversation, Spencer said he'd pick up takeout food for dinner the next night and asked me what I would like to eat. I told him I liked Chinese food. I listed off about ten items so he would have plenty of options to choose from. When we finally hung up, I couldn't wait for the next day.

But first, I immediately opened my dating app. It shows you who your mutual Facebook friends are, and I saw that Spencer knew a girl named Mary Kate who I had grown up with in the dance studio. Just to be extra cautious, I'd get the scoop from her before going to his place.

I texted Mary Kate: "Mary Kate, you know Spencer?"

"Yeah, he's my next-door neighbor," she replied.

What?! I thought. *How have we never met?!* "Am I safe going to his apartment?"

"Oh, yeah, you're good. He's a cop, and he comes from a good family. You'll be fine."

I thanked her for her insight and tried to sleep.

The next morning, I practically jumped out of bed. Before I could meet Spencer, I first had to attend an event as Miss Warner Robins. It was a fairy princess dress-up party, so I would be reading books to a group of little girls. I'm all about kids. I love them. But on this particular day, all I could think about was meeting Spencer. As soon as my appearance was over, I got into my car, took my crown and sash off, touched up my makeup, and sped over to his apartment.

Before I arrived, he had told me to pull into the driveway and park in front of the barn. When I got there, I didn't see a vehicle. Instead, there was an enormous house and kids playing in the yard. *What in the world?* I thought. *Why are there children here? This can't be his house.* A woman walked over to my car and said, "Hi, can I help you?"

"Hi, I'm here to meet Spencer."

"Oh yeah, he told us a girl would be dropping by today. He should be here soon."

"Thanks," I said. *Great. I beat him here,* I thought. *I hate when that happens.*

After a few minutes, Spencer pulled up in his Ford Toyota Tacoma. I purposely tried not to catch a glimpse of him as he drove past me and parked. I wanted the perfect mental picture of the first time I saw him. When he got out of his truck, I was blown away. He looked even better in person. He wore a backward baseball cap, a polo, and jeans. I liked his laidback but slightly polished look. Spencer grabbed the Chinese takeout and opened my car door for me. Then he offered me his hand and helped me out of my car like a perfect southern gentleman. He told me I looked beautiful, and we hugged. I swooned.

"Alright. Let's head up," he said. Spencer explained he was renting out the guesthouse of the family who lived in the main house. We walked past a chicken coop and climbed the steps to his apartment. As soon as we got inside, I took a seat on a stool at the kitchen counter while he unpacked the Chinese food. He had bought every single dish I had mentioned!

"Why did you buy so much?" I asked, shocked.

"You said you wanted all of this," he said, smiling.

"I just told you what I liked!" I laughed. "I can't eat all of that!" It was a sweet gesture regardless.

"Oh, before I forget," he started to say and walked over to me. Then he kissed me—right then and there. "Didn't want to do that in front of the kids."

Whoa. Immediate fireworks. *This is it,* I thought. *This is the guy.*

We ate, talked, and watched a movie on the couch. We held hands, and it felt like we had been dating forever. I was perfectly comfortable. As the night wound down, he looked at me and asked, "How does a guy get you to be his girlfriend?"

"Well, you just ask me."

"Will you be my girlfriend?"

"Yes, I would love to be your girlfriend." I was surprised and honored that he wanted to commit so quickly—especially since I could tell he was probably popular with the ladies.

"Oh, but first I should probably break it off with the other guys I've been messaging, so we can have a clean start," I said.

He agreed and said, "I should do that too."

It was getting late, so we said our goodbyes for the night. The next day, I texted, called, and met up with guys who I had been getting to know to tell them I had found someone. They were all surprisingly cool with it and very understanding. Hester, my mentor for Miss Georgia, was not. When I told her about Spencer, I said, "I met a guy I really like, and I'm going to start dating him."

"You don't need to be dating anybody," she snapped. "You just need to focus on getting ready for Miss Georgia. You need to chill out on dating until after the competition." She had seen me go through Edgar, Rex, and Brad, and apparently, she thought they were all distracting me from focusing on pageant prep.

"This guy is different, Hester. I know how that sounds, but I'm going to date him."

"No, you're not," she said. "You are not dating him. No more dating."

I wanted to say: *You don't get to tell me who I can and cannot date.* But my parents raised me to be respectful, so I kept my mouth shut and decided I'd just have to keep my relationship with Spencer a secret from Hester.

Before Spencer and I met for our second date, we were officially boyfriend and girlfriend. On our second date, we were sitting on the couch in his apartment and hanging out. He leaned over to kiss me but stopped and said, "Betty . . . I love you." I was shocked and overwhelmed, but I felt the exact same way. It was so soon, and I didn't think love at first sight was real. I leaned in to kiss him, but he stopped me again, put his hands on either side of my face, and said, "No, I'm really in love with you."

"I love you too," I said.

By our third date, we were talking about marriage. It was all happening insanely fast, and I had never moved this quickly with any other guy I had dated. To say "I love you" was a huge deal to me. But we still felt we had to keep our relationship quiet because of Hester. That meant no sharing photos of ourselves or making our relationship known on social media.

I did tell my mom, though. I told her I had met Spencer on a dating app; he was a cop, and I was going to marry him.

"Oh, Betty. I can't believe you're doing this. Hester said—"

"Mom, I don't care what Hester says," I told her. "Spencer's the one." I left out the part about how we had already exchanged "I love yous." I didn't want to scare her because I knew how fast we were moving. But to me and Spencer, our relationship was moving at just the right pace. We knew it was fast, but we were certain of each other.

"I know, I know," my mom said. "You think he's the one, but you really need to focus on getting ready for Miss Georgia."

"I *am* going to focus on it, but I'm also going to have a really awesome boyfriend alongside me."

"Then you need to be honest with Hester."

I knew my mom was right, so I broke the news to Hester. She was disappointed, but she said, "If you really think he's the one, then I guess you can be with him. But he better not distract you." Once Hester knew, Spencer and I made our relationship Facebook official, which was a big deal in 2015. I was so excited to share who he was with all of my friends and family. No more keeping our relationship a secret!

Then, on my fourth date with Spencer, we were headed to a pizza place for dinner. The sun was setting, and I started imagining our future together. But I quickly realized much of it was riding on what happened at Miss Georgia, which was just a few months away.

"Hey, we need to talk," I said.

"Uh oh," Spencer glanced at me sideways from the driver's seat. No one ever wants to hear those words.

"I just want you to know if I do well and win Miss Georgia, then I'll be Miss Georgia for a year. That means I'm going to be traveling a lot and doing tons of appearances, and that could be really hard for us. And then, if I were to win Miss America, and I know that's a long shot and probably won't happen, but I would be gone for an entire year." Spencer was the one God sent for me, and I wanted to be honest with him and lay it all out on the table. I thought he should know exactly what he could be getting himself into.

"Well, count me in." Spencer didn't even hesitate.

I couldn't believe his response. I thought maybe I wasn't clear enough, so I tried to be even more plain about what I meant: "I just want to give you a chance to get out before you're into something you didn't sign up for."

"No, I'm not going anywhere. I'm in this. I love you," he said. "I don't care what happens in your life; I'm going to be part of it with you."

I couldn't believe how unfazed he was. My future was unknown, but he believed in me. I was on cloud nine. This guy was the love of my life, and he was ready to stand by my side and walk down whatever crazy journey might lay ahead of us. I knew it was time he met my parents.

Given how conservative my parents are, I was a little nervous to introduce Spencer to them. He had tattoos. A lot of them. I took Spencer to the Cantrell Center, and since my mom and dad were in the midst of their divorce, we went to their separate offices—first my mom's and then my dad's. They both seemed to like him, but I could tell they were also hesitant. Some of his tattoos were visible, and they could see he was a little rough around the edges. I knew it was going to take some time for them to see past his tattoos, but Spencer was used to people's uncertainty about him. What mattered most was that my parents were happy for me to have a supportive, respectful, and caring boyfriend.

Even though I was working harder than ever in my pageant preparation, things with Hester started to get worse. Nothing I did was good enough for her. When I told her I wasn't going to have time to write one of her assigned papers, she responded, "You know what? That kind of laziness is going to lead to your inevitable failure at Miss Georgia." If I forgot to complete a task, she'd say something similar. I once sent her a picture of myself in a swimsuit that I was considering wearing for Miss Georgia, and she wrote back, "I'm seeing a little bit of cellulite on your thighs there, Betty. I think you should probably hit the gym a little bit harder. You're not looking as good as you could."

Not only was I not good enough, but I was also not grateful enough. My mom and I would often travel to Atlanta for pageant-related work. While there, we'd visit Thomas for my voice coaching, do mock interviews with Chuck, prepare my pageant wardrobe, and visit gown shops. Since Hester lived in Atlanta, she would offer for us to stay at her house, so we did, but she made sure we were always aware of just how generous she was. She'd remind us how we weren't having to pay for a hotel, food, or her coaching: "You should be grateful I'm doing all of this for free and out of the goodness of my heart." We offered to pay her for her coaching, and when she declined, we tried to express our appreciation with gifts. My mom and I continuously thanked her, but we slowly started to realize our gratitude would never be enough.

I found myself crying all the time. I no longer felt like Hester was building me up but tearing me down. I got to a place in my head where I didn't even want to compete anymore. I was doing hundreds of tasks, including working with a designer, Jay Reynolds, to design my own evening gown. My relationship with Hester became toxic and needed to end, so I broke it off with her shortly before my second running at Miss Georgia. I told her I couldn't do it anymore. She was working me too hard, and I felt bullied. My confidence was taking a hit, and I wasn't willing to continue feeling the way that I did. Hester did not take it well. She began texting me, telling me how ungrateful I was and that I didn't deserve to win Miss Georgia. I knew I made the right call by ending my relationship with her.

June arrived, and I headed to Miss Georgia with my mom, dad, and Spencer to support me. My week there had gone great, although I didn't see myself as a frontrunner. At the prelims, they announced the winners of the overall talent, evening gown, interview, and swimsuit awards. I won overall talent with my opera piece, "Tu, Tu, Piccolo Iddio." Then, I won overall evening gown with my custom-designed gown! I even won overall interview, which shocked me.

All the runners up were named, and it was down to one other girl and me. We stood face to face and held hands. There's an old pageant myth that the girl whose hands are on top will be named the winner. I looked down at our hands and saw hers were on top. It got into my head for just a second, and I feared I'd lost. But I quickly rerouted my brain and reminded myself that the results were in God's hands. *God, please let this be part of your plan for me*, I prayed.

The other girl was called as first runner-up, and I was crowned Miss Georgia 2015! I couldn't believe it. Even though I had made more friends during my second time competing for Miss Georgia, not everyone was happy I had won. In fact, I received a lot of backlash. I was the new girl who hadn't paid her dues yet. I later found out some of the girls backstage were saying, "Ugh. Anybody but Betty Cantrell." According to them, other girls deserved it more than me.

As sad as it is, stereotypes sometimes hold true. It hurt my feelings, and I was later torn apart on the anonymous online pageant chat boards. It wore me down and made me feel awful about myself. So many people in the pageant community and in my own state didn't support me. But I knew I had to ignore it as best as I could and continue pushing forward. I was still proud of myself despite the people who tried to bring me down.

Right after I was crowned, I attended the winner's reception, where I took more pictures than I could count and met more people than I could remember. Then, I met the board of directors for the Miss Georgia Pageant. This was a huge deal because they're basically untouchable. Contestants aren't allowed to interact with the board because of potential conflicts of interests, but now they were all on my team! I also got to spend a few minutes with my family and Spencer. We shared our excitement, but I was quickly brought to the presidential suite at the Marriott for the night. I'd never stayed in such a fancy room before!

The next morning, the board sat me down to discuss the year ahead of me. One of the first things they told me was that I was to have no contact with Hester. This was such a huge relief, and I was so grateful. They saw how toxic her involvement had been, and they were putting a stop to it. Hester later sent me a nasty text telling me how she hoped I wouldn't do well at Miss America, but I was not going to let her words affect me. They didn't matter now. I had a supportive family, boyfriend, and board of directors who were cheering me on as I was about to take one step closer to my dreams.

When I think back on my road to Miss America, I can't help but wonder where I would be today if I hadn't listened to my mom and given pageants a chance. What if I had been too scared to try? Failure is disappointing—each and every time. But what if I had given up after the first, second, third, or even fourth time I didn't win a pageant? What if I had chosen to stay in college and play it safe despite knowing it wasn't my purpose? What if I had gone to realty school? Or what if I'd believed Hester when she said I didn't have what it took?

I was just a normal, everyday girl who grew up on a farm, but what I lacked in experience I made up for with hard work and faith. It didn't matter who thought I couldn't make it or why or what they thought I *should* do. God gave me a love for singing and performing, and I was ready to turn those passions into my reality. I was honored to be crowned Miss Georgia, and I couldn't wait to compete at Miss America and give it my all!

CHAPTER 7

A Long Way from Georgia

The preparation for Miss America was far more intensive than the prep for Miss Georgia, and I didn't have much time to get ready. I was crowned Miss Georgia in June, and Miss America was to take place in September. That meant I only had a few months to prepare for a pageant that most girls spend their entire pageant careers preparing for. Fortunately, I had the incredible Miss Georgia team to support me, and they were, without a doubt, my saving grace.

One huge misconception about pageants is that they are strictly about appearances—the big hair, the overdone makeup, and the expensive gowns, but they're *so* much more than that. In fact, most of the more intensive work I did was to prepare for the swimsuit, talent, and interview portions of the competition. And my board had my back!

The board set me up with a personal trainer in Atlanta named Stephen Smith. The workouts were grueling, full body types of workouts—weightlifting, resistance training, and running. I *hate* running. It was a two-hour commute one way, and I was training three to four times a week. If Spencer wasn't working, he'd sometimes go with me and work out alongside me but do his own thing.

Thomas and I had been hoping and praying since our first session together that I would get to bring "Tu, Tu, Piccolo Iddio" to the Miss America stage. It was finally happening! We both had such a love for its drama and knew how it should be performed. We'd have weekly sessions during which I would sing it over and over and over for him. Then we'd brainstorm ideas for choreography—how and when I'd move my hands or work my dress while I sang. Then I'd perform it again, and he'd offer me his critiques and corrections.

And finally, I did several mock interviews. The interview portion is the first phase of the Miss America pageant, and it will make or break you. It's your only opportunity to communicate privately with the judges, so you have to make a good impression. In order to do that, you have to keep up with current events and have thoughtful, articulate responses prepared for whatever questions the panel of judges may throw at you. If you have no clue what you're talking about or you're struggling to come up with an answer, the judges will weed you out right then and there.

I did around a dozen mock interviews to make sure I was ready. The Miss Georgia board would gather a group of notable people from our community (former pageant winners, news anchors, lawyers, etc.) to serve as judges, and they would ask me questions just like the real thing. That was the best way to prep. We also went to a theater with a real stage and prepared for the on-stage question portion of Miss America. The board members would sit in the audience and pretend to be judges. They would ask me questions on current events and then time my answers. We did this over and over until they felt I was prepared for anything they could throw at me. The last thing anyone wants is to get eliminated right at the start of the competition.

My schedule was intense that summer, and those three months came and went in what felt like a blink of an eye. Not only was I preparing for Miss America, but I was also having to live out my role as Miss Georgia at the same time. If I wasn't attending an event or making an appearance as Miss Georgia, I was prepping for Miss America. I was working really hard, but I honestly loved every minute of it. I had so much support from the entire Miss Georgia board, and I wanted to win for them. And I desperately wanted to be the girl who brought the Miss America title home to our state, which hadn't won the crown in sixty-three years.

I knew I was an underdog, and sure, I wanted to win for myself, but mostly I wanted to win for every little girl who felt like she couldn't be Miss America just because she wasn't a "pageant girl." I truly felt like God lit a fire in me to be this role model and to serve as an inspiration to young people. I wanted to show them that if I could do it, so could they. The pressure was mounting, and soon it was time to start packing my bags.

But packing for Miss America requires more than just throwing some clothes into a couple of suitcases. It's a sport in and of itself. The pageant and all of the associated events take place over a span of two weeks, and you have to plan out *everything* you are going to wear and when—every single outfit for every single day. I tried on each outfit at the home of my Miss Georgia director, Greg Blazer. Together, we planned out the shoes, jewelry, accessories, hairstyles, and makeup for each ensemble. Not one detail was ignored. Once we were satisfied with my wardrobe, we carefully organized the outfits and packed them into large, plastic containers. We even wrote down the details for every outfit so I wouldn't forget anything.

We shipped the containers directly to Boardwalk Hall in Atlantic City, New Jersey, where the pageant takes place. The Miss America Organization, or MAO, has very strict rules about pageant wardrobes in that everything must be either shipped directly to the venue or taken directly to the venue by the contestant herself. This is to avoid any kind of additional coaching, bias, or cheating. For this same reason, MAO also has strict policies about who contestants are permitted to interact with during the two weeks of competition and what those interactions can look like. For example, if I had forgotten a pair of earrings, and my mom was in Atlantic City, she still would have had to ship them directly to Boardwalk Hall. All of it may sound crazy and tedious, but it's also understandable. The organization is committed to keeping the pageant as fair as possible to ensure every contestant has an equal shot at the title.

Another common misconception is that pageants are unfair because only young women who come from wealthy backgrounds can afford to participate. In other words, the more money you have, the better your chances are at winning. You can afford a nicer gown, all of the clothing and accessories you need, and the best coaches to get you ready. And don't get me wrong. It *is* expensive; there's no way around it. But! You can be creative and resourceful. For example, I did some modeling work for Jay Reynolds and, in exchange, he gave me a deal on the gown of my dreams. I paid only $200 for a designer gown while many contestants paid thousands. I also recycled my outfits instead of starting from scratch with each and every pageant. A lot of boards require their state winner to purchase an all-new wardrobe, but my board respected my love for my evening gown and other outfits. The only new outfits I purchased for Miss America were my swimsuit and interview dress. The truth is that you *don't* have to come from money to compete for Miss America.

Finally, the day to leave for Atlantic City came. This would be my first ever experience of flying alone. I was crazy stressed about getting through security, finding my gate, and trusting that my two suitcases full of makeup and accessories would safely arrive in baggage claim. My mom and the board of directors reassured me it would all work out just fine as we drove to the airport together. Looking back, I can't help but laugh because now I'm a total pro when it comes to traveling. I can lead you to each and every Chick-fil-A in the Atlanta airport and probably any other restaurant you may be looking for. But at the time, I was a nervous wreck.

When we arrived at the Hartsfield-Jackson Atlanta International Airport, I was in full hair and makeup, wearing black, high-waisted pants and an orange bodysuit to represent Mercer's colors. I very much looked the part of the pageant girl. I checked myself in before waving goodbye to everyone. Once I made it through security, I was on a mission to find my gate. It was a much easier task than my anxious brain had anticipated, and I silently thanked God as soon as I found it. Then, as I sat near my gate waiting for my flight to board, I saw Miss Iowa.

"Oh my gosh, I'm so happy to see you!" I exclaimed as I hugged her. She had a connecting flight in Atlanta, and since Atlantic City doesn't have an airport, we were boarding the same flight to Philadelphia, where we'd catch a shuttle to Atlantic City. I was so grateful and relieved to see a familiar face, and her presence alone was a huge comfort. I was flying first class, compliments of the Miss Georgia board, which always purchases first-class tickets for their winners. I had never flown first class before, so it was a huge deal to me and also kind of intimidating. The flight went great, though, and when we landed, Miss Iowa and I had the privilege of meeting the pilot and sitting in the pilot's seat. We put on our crowns and sashes and took a few pictures of us wearing the captain's hat, which was fun.

When we got to baggage claim, we were met by two Miss America security guards. Contestants were assigned into groups of ten, and each group had a designated security guard and two hostesses. The hostesses would help to keep us on schedule and remind us of what we needed to pack for the day. They also accompanied us to and from our hotels. Each group stayed at a different hotel within Atlantic City, and my group was staying at the Trump Taj Mahal (now the Hard Rock Hotel & Casino). Our security guard was Chris, and he and I quickly became BFFs. He always had us laughing and helped keep us calm before competing. Like everyone had assured me, my suitcases arrived! Chris and the other security guard hauled our luggage off the conveyor belt and escorted us to the shuttle that read "Miss America" on the side.

We arrived at the Trump Taj Mahal, which was a hotel and casino and unlike any hotel I had ever seen before. I'd never even been inside a casino! Three enormous chandeliers hung in the lobby, and everything was accented in gold. It was a lot to take in, and my eyes had to have been the size of saucers as I gazed around. All of the contestants checked in, and we dropped our things off in our rooms. Two contestants were assigned to each room. Then the organization took us out to our first dinner at an Italian restaurant called Boca. They serve the best coffee I've ever had in my life, and Boca later became my favorite spot to eat whenever my travels brought me back to Atlantic City.

The entire first week of Miss America consists of rehearsals and appearances. Each day, we would rehearse in Boardwalk Hall where the live pageant would be held and televised on the final night. Here, we learned where to walk and stand and what to do for the opening number. The opening number had all the contestants enter the stage, perform a little bit of simple dance choreography, and then share a rehearsed opening statement. The opening statement included a catchy phrase about your state, your name, and your title. Mine was: "If you want to get to heaven, you have to go through Atlanta, home of the world's most beautiful airport. I'm Miss Georgia, Betty Cantrell."

These rehearsals often lasted hours, but they were surprisingly fun. The staff is awesome, and we all goofed off quite a bit. We didn't have to wear full pageant gear for them either. In fact, most of us wore athleisure outfits of leggings or shorts, comfortable tops, and athletic jackets. The music selections made rehearsals even more fun. It really makes all the difference when you're walking across a stage in a swimsuit and need an extra confidence boost.

After rehearsals, we would do our hair and makeup, change into our pageant outfits, and attend events all around Atlantic City. Everywhere we went, we were evaluated by Miss America hosts, board members, and directors, so we always wanted to dress to impress. We did appearances with the Children's Miracle Network Hospital and the Atlantic City Rescue Mission, as well as other local events.

Then one day during that first week, I had a morning I will never forget. It was a total disaster. The first thing on our agenda that morning was to film the opening segment of the telecast in which we introduce ourselves. The telecast would then air on the final night of the pageant, so it was a big deal and easily one of the days you wanted to look your best. Somehow, my alarm failed to go off. Instead, I woke up to the sound of the hostess knocking on our door, saying, "Alright, ladies! Time to go!"

What in the world? How did this happen? I panicked. Getting ready for these events is a whole production of hair, makeup, and careful styling. I'm used to taking my time—sometimes up to two hours. But that morning, I had only minutes to gather my things and get out the door. With tears rolling down my cheeks, I leapt out of bed. For some reason, my roommate didn't even consider waking me up. It wasn't her responsibility, of course, but had our roles been reversed that morning, I absolutely would have had her back and woken her up. I was hurt but had no time to talk about it or waste time feeling upset at her.

I threw on my dress and packed my other outfits for the day. I tossed my makeup into a bag and glued my false eyelashes on in what had to have been record time. My makeup looked like I did it on a moving bus . . . because I did! I had to apply it en route to our location for the shoot, and the bus offered little to no lighting. Makeup was spilling out of my bag with every bump and turn. I was borrowing makeup from other people. Panicked and frazzled, I gathered my hair into a half-up, half-down style, but it was all over the place. I looked truly awful. I was embarrassed for myself and for the Miss Georgia board. I wanted so badly to represent them in the best way possible in everything I did.

The whole experience felt like it was straight out of a nightmare. I told Spencer all about it over the phone that night and warned him to be prepared for how awful I looked. I also called the board to warn them too. I couldn't help but cry on the phone with them as I tried to explain what had gone wrong. They were, of course, understanding. At this point, we were more like family. They encouraged me to not let one day get me down and to stay positive. When I saw the telecast, everyone's hair looked a little disheveled because it had been so windy that day. Regardless, I was still deeply upset and felt like I had let everyone down.

Thankfully, no other day was that bad. In fact, one of the best days was a trip to New York City for a *Good Morning America* appearance. It also happened to be my twenty-first birthday, and we had to wake up around 3:30 that morning. It was a very, very long day, but it was so much fun to be on national television with all the other contestants.

And that night in New York City was magical. It sounds corny, I know, but we were treated to a fancy dinner at a trendy restaurant in the heart of the city. Unbeknownst to me, the girls had told the chef it was my birthday, and the server brought out a giant ice cream dessert dripping in fudge and lit with one candle. The girls sang "Happy Birthday," and I was overwhelmed with emotion. I couldn't believe I was competing in Miss America, celebrating a birthday surprise, and enjoying this insanely delicious meal in New York City of all places. I had come a long way from Middle Georgia!

When week two rolled around, we could feel the intensity shift in a big way. The competition suddenly got real. Interviews were the first stage of the competition, which account for 25 percent of your overall score. All of the contestants did considerable amounts of research on the judges once we were told who they would be. That information helped us find ways to relate to them, and it gave us a better idea of what to expect from the conversations. Like I said before, the interview is so, so important.

The sequence of the interviews was randomly determined by a lottery system, and the way it unfolded left me with two spots to choose from: first or second. Neither were ideal, and no one wants to interview first, so I chose to interview second. A lot of people already counted me out of the competition strictly because of my interview placement. They assumed I'd be forgotten for having interviewed so early. But I didn't really mind having to interview second. I was actually kind of relieved that I wouldn't have to wait around and listen to how other girls' interviews went and then inevitably compare my experience to theirs. I just wanted to get it over with.

Miss Kansas, who interviewed first, exited the interview room looking content and at peace. *Okay,* I thought, *I got this. I can do this.* I felt calm, anxious, and excited all at the same time. Adrenaline rushed through my body as I walked toward the doors. I was in full interview mode.

"This is Miss Georgia, Betty Cantrell," an MAO staff member announced as I entered the room. I immediately made eye contact with each judge and greeted them with a "good morning" as I took my position at the podium. I thought about Sam Haskell, the CEO and president of MAO at the time, who we were notified beforehand would be watching us on a monitor from an adjoining room. He couldn't sit in with the judges because it would be a conflict of interest. By watching from a separate room, any potential for bias or favor was eliminated. Just the thought of him watching from the next room was nerve-wracking!

I approached the designated podium and said, "Thank you so much for having me today!" Now, I'm a rambler. I could talk forever. But in pageant interviews, you don't want your responses to last too long. You want to get through as many questions as possible; that way, the judges have the very best opportunity to get to know you. This was something I had to work really hard on during my mock interviews. I had to learn how and when to cut myself off and concentrate on saying only what I needed to say.

As soon as I introduced myself, the judges started firing questions. They asked me questions about my résumé, platform, and lots of current events. I ended up getting through quite a few. One of the judges was a fan of Broadway, and another judge was Greek, so I felt especially fortunate to have things in common with them.

"What is one of your bad habits?"

"I bite my nails," I answered. "Look," I said, showing them my right hand, "I had fake nails, but I've even picked off one of *them*!" They laughed, and I breathed a sigh of relief.

All that remained of my interview was the thirty-second closing. The interviews are timed at ten minutes, and the last thirty seconds are reserved for contestants to share anything they want the judges to know about them that wasn't already asked. I used this time to talk about growing up in a double-wide trailer on a farm. I expressed an understanding of what the job of Miss America requires and my confidence in fulfilling the responsibilities. I also acknowledged my lack of experience in pageants and explained how that actually gave me a fresh perspective.

Overall, I was really happy with how my interview went. I felt like I remained true to myself throughout the discussion, which was hugely important to me. I wasn't a traditional pageant girl, and I wasn't going to pretend like I was. If I was going to win, I was going to win as Betty Cantrell, the aspiring singer and actress who grew up running barefoot through the fields of her farm, attending church with her family every Sunday, and watching episodes of *The Andy Griffith Show* on repeat.

Then just a few days into the second week, I had another setback. I woke up one morning with a horribly sore throat, a stuffy nose, and an enormous amount of pressure in my head. Everything you don't want as a singer. I visited the doctor on staff, and he confirmed I had a sinus infection. The infection meant my vocal cords were swollen, making me sound hoarse, and the congestion made my voice more nasally. I was devastated and deeply worried about singing for the talent portion of the competition. How was I going to perform to the best of my abilities when I felt like shards of broken glass were sliding down my throat every time I swallowed? He prescribed a Z-PAK and gave me a shot in my arm. It was unusually painful and made my entire arm tender and sore for the rest of the week.

To make matters worse, visitation with friends and family wasn't allowed until the preliminaries began, so I could only talk to Spencer and my family over the phone even though they were already in Atlantic City. Spencer was staying with my dad and Mikey at the Marriott, and one night we discovered we could see each other's hotel rooms from our windows but from far away. Now and then, Spencer would shine the flashlight on his phone in my direction, and I would shine mine back. It was a small gesture, but it eased the loneliness that crept in from time to time. And I found it sweet and romantic. He would also take walks on the boardwalk in the evening and flash his light at my window.

Miss America is an intense competition to begin with, and when you couple that intensity with the natural isolation that comes with rehearsals and appearances that keep your mind in competition mode day in and day out, it starts to wear on your spirit. If I hadn't had the support of Spencer and my family, I might have lost my mind! I prayed continually throughout those two weeks, asking God for strength, resilience, and humility.

Sleep was rare too. We usually had to be up in the mornings around 6:00 in order to have time to prepare for the day of rehearsals and events, and then we usually didn't get back to the hotel until 10:00 or 11:00 at night. The exhaustion was setting in deeply by week two, but because that was competition week, we had to push through. I suspect the adrenaline and excitement kept us going more than anything.

One night, Spencer and I were talking on the phone as he walked along the boardwalk. I was telling him about my fears if I won and my fears if I didn't. He stopped me and said, "Whether you win or not, I'm going to be here. But I know that you're going to win, and I want you to win! I want you to do your best. Your dreams are my dreams, Betty."

I'd never been more sure that Spencer was the one for me. "Your dreams are my dreams" became our phrase for each other, and we started using #ydamd on all of our social media posts. I felt like the luckiest girl in the world going into the final days of the competition knowing he was behind me 100 percent.

Preliminaries came next and took place over a span of three nights. The prelims determine the top fifteen contenders who are later announced at the beginning of the live telecast. The interviews had taken place on Sunday and Monday, which meant Tuesday, Wednesday, and Thursday were the talent, swimsuit, evening gown, and on-stage question prelims. Three groups of contestants performed each night for each respective category. After the night's competition, the contestants would go back onto the stage, and the preliminary winners of the night were announced for the swimsuit and talent portions. There were no evening gown or on-stage question winners during the prelims.

With everything that was going on, I couldn't wait for visitation with friends and family that first night of preliminaries. Any friends, family, and state board members of the titleholders who purchased a pass to attend the prelims had the opportunity to visit with contestants for twenty-five minutes at the end of each night. It had been a week and a half since I had seen Spencer or my family, and I couldn't wait to see them.

"You know you're going to win," Spencer told me when I saw him that first night. "I'm telling you right now that you are going to win."

His unwavering confidence in me and his unconditional support astounded me, and I think my family really grew to love him because they were witnessing firsthand just how much he cared about me.

On the third and final night of the prelims, I performed my talent. It was the most important category to me, and I *so* wanted to be a talent prelim winner. I felt okay about my performance but knew it definitely wasn't my best because of my sinus infection. I prayed and prayed as I stood on stage waiting to hear the winners for the night. When my name was announced as the winner of the talent portion, I was beyond excited! I couldn't wait to see my family, friends, Spencer, and especially Thomas! *And* I would get a lei from the Miss Hawaii board!

During visitation, the Miss Hawaii board gave out leis to the girls who won talent and swimsuit each night and sang a Hawaiian song to celebrate. I wanted one of those leis so badly! They were real, legit flowers and absolutely gorgeous. When they placed the lei around my neck, it was definitely one of the highlights for me up to that point!

It was hardly a surprise when Miss Hawaii was later voted Miss Congeniality by the contestants. She was the absolute sweetest, as was her board, and she even planted trees in Hawaii for each contestant before coming to the competition. We all adored her.

After the preliminary nights were finished, we still had to get through Friday and Saturday before the live telecast on Sunday night. Friday's major event was the Show Me Your Shoes Parade. It's a huge tradition in Atlantic City where the Miss America contestants ride on the back of convertibles, show off their elaborately decorated shoes, and wave at the crowd. Each of the contestants decorates a shoe and wears a costume, and at the end of the parade, the shoes are put on display for the crowd. The idea is for the contestant to theme their shoe in a way that represents their state. Naturally, many former Miss Georgias themed their shoes around a peach or their university in Georgia, but I wanted to do something different.

Since my talent piece was from *Madame Butterfly*, I fashioned my shoe to resemble a butterfly, and I dressed like a butterfly. I wore a custom-made, hot pink jumpsuit with big, matching wings made of papier-mâché made by Scott Marchbanks of Frills by Scott, a boutique in Statesboro, Georgia. My shoes also had a small pair of butterfly wings on the toe, and the heels were covered in silver rhinestones. The couple driving the convertible I rode on was so sweet. They had thick New Jersey accents and kept telling me, "You're going to win! You're our girl!"

The procession is in alphabetical order of the states, and year after year, rain pours during this parade. It never fails, and the parade is never canceled on account of the weather. Since my wings were made of papier-mâché, I anxiously waited for the rain to dissolve them. Sure enough, it started to pour toward the end of the parade.

My wings were inevitably ruined, but I only had a short distance left to travel before reaching the end of the parade route. I was spared getting soaked like the girls at the back of the line. I felt so sorry for them, and poor Miss Wisconsin and Miss Wyoming received no mercy. We were all freezing cold by the end of it. Nevertheless, the parade was a fun experience, and it was cool to be part of a beloved Atlantic City tradition.

Saturday was strictly booked for rehearsals for Sunday night. In order to rehearse what would take place on Sunday night with the top fifteen finalists, we had the option of participating as a "fake" finalist for rehearsal's sake. You would draw a number out of a bowl to determine who would play the parts of the finalists. That way, we could all watch and see what we would need to do if we did, in fact, make the top fifteen.

I was honestly a little weirded out by that, so I opted to sit on stage and watch instead, and I'm so glad I did. By this point, we were all exhausted, and the generous girls who did volunteer ended up having to do a lot more work that day. So we sat and observed and memorized what we'd need to do if we were lucky enough to be placed in the top fifteen for the final night. The MAO team is really good about not announcing a first runner-up or a winner during rehearsals because it makes everyone uncomfortable. Instead, they have a running joke where they crown Stacy, the choreographer, as the new Miss America. It lightens the mood since pretty much every contestant is feeling tense and tired.

People often ask me if I ever had a ritual I would perform before going on stage. It's a common question because a lot of girls do. Some wear a special piece of jewelry or perform some kind of ritualistic warm-up routine. But I honestly never did anything like that. All I ever did was pray. Prayer was my go-to practice any and every time I competed.

As I prayed that night before bed, I asked God to calm my nerves and help me do my best. I asked him to be near me and give me peace. And that's exactly what I felt going into the final night when Miss America 2016 would be broadcast live across the US and the new Miss America would be crowned.

All of my hard work had led up to these final few hours. I had given it my all. I knew I had done everything I possibly could to make a good impression on the judges, and all I could do from that point on was give it all to God. I was ready to see if my name would appear in the top fifteen contestants and if I would have the chance—my dream—of singing on national television and ultimately competing for the title of Miss America 2016.

CHAPTER 8

There She Is, Miss America

On the morning of September 15, 2015, I woke up still feeling sick from my sinus infection. It was the final night of the Miss America pageant and the celebration of the Miss America Organization's ninety-fifth, hallmark anniversary. It was also the culmination of all my hard work. An all-new panel of celebrity judges would use their fresh perspectives to determine who would become the next Miss America. Vanessa Williams, the 1984 Miss America winner and the first African-American woman to hold the title, was our head judge, and the other judges included Brett Eldredge, Taya Kyle, Danica McKellar, Kevin O'Leary, Amy Purdy, and Zendaya. As soon as we arrived at Boardwalk Hall that morning for prep and rehearsals, I started chugging Emergen-C and hot tea and doing everything I could to make my throat feel better. I was going to have to rely on pure adrenaline to get me through the day and night.

The telecast always begins with the announcement of the top fifteen contenders who are still in the running for the crown. Those who don't make the top fifteen must remain in the dresses they wore for the opening number and watch the entire competition unfold from the side of the stage, or the "Loser Lounge" as we contestants called it. It's brutal. The top fifteen compete all over again in the same categories from the prelims: swimsuit, evening gown, talent, and on-stage question.

A huge dressing room backstage held all of the contestants while we got ourselves ready. This was the first (and last) year in which contestants were prohibited from bringing people in to help with hair and makeup, which gave all of us one more thing to stress about. We each had a small table to ourselves, and on the table was a mirror with lights. Girls were curling and teasing their hair and carefully swirling makeup brushes across their eyelids. Others were stretching or, like me, warming up their vocal cords.

It was awkward to warm up as a singer because it's not as subtle as a dancer quietly stretching. There's also the reality that you may not even get the opportunity to perform your talent, but it's better to be prepared than not in the event your name is called. I had to sing "la, la, la, la, la, la, la" over and over again—and loudly. The energy among the contestants was calm and focused, so I did my best not to irritate the girls around me. But I'm not sure how successful I was. It's hard not to be on edge under that amount of stress, and we were all feeling it.

The telecast started, and for the opening number, some of us danced down the aisles in the audience to get to the stage. I danced down one of them, smiling and waving at the crowd. Once we were all in our places on stage, we reached for the hands of the girls standing beside us. It was time to announce the top fifteen.

Since the swimsuit phase takes place immediately after the announcement of the top fifteen, the hostesses backstage are informed of which girls are advancing in the competition just before the telecast begins. They then bring the swimsuits and accessories belonging to the remaining contestants to a small room backstage for the girls to do a quick change. As I stood there waiting, my eyes glanced to the wings of the stage. I wondered if my stuff was back there. *Please God, if this is your will for me, let it happen,* I prayed.

"Miss Tennessee, Hannah Robison!" The first name called wasn't mine. And neither was the second, third, fourth, fifth, or sixth. I concentrated on being happy for my friends and celebrating their accomplishment. I didn't want to focus on the fact that my name hadn't been called; that way of thinking was neither productive nor positive. About halfway through the top fifteen, it was time for a commercial break. We all let our big, plastered smiles fall and took deep breaths. I looked to where I knew my family and Spencer were sitting and waved. The anticipation was almost nauseating. I stood there and just kept praying, *God, please let this be your will for me.*

We returned from the break and hosts Chris Harrison and Brooke Burke continued to call out names—none of them mine. *Maybe they did forget me because I interviewed second,* I thought. *There are fifty-two of us, and that's a lot of contestants.* They announced number twelve, and again, it wasn't me. I was preparing myself not to make it: *It's going to be okay,* I assured myself.

"Lucky number thirteen, Miss Georgia!"

My knees buckled, but I hurried to the front of the stage. As I waved at the audience, my earring fell out and onto the stage. *Oh my gosh, right now!?* I hadn't been instructed on what to do if something like this happened. *Do I pick it up or leave it?* I wondered. I didn't want anyone else to slip or step on it, so I bent down and picked it up. I held the earring in my hand and continued to wave before rushing to the side of the stage where we were instructed to stand as they finished calling out numbers fourteen and fifteen. I hugged the girls around me before taking my place in line next to them.

My heart went out to the girls who hadn't made it. I can only imagine how it must have felt not only to learn you wouldn't be moving ahead in the competition, but also to learn that on live, national television. I think it's safe to say that most people would rather not cry in public let alone on TV. That could not have been easy—especially for the girls who had been preparing for Miss America nearly their entire lives. So many of those girls had become dear friends of mine, and my heart just broke for them. It was a bittersweet moment.

But I wasn't able to dwell there for long because we were immediately rushed backstage to prepare for swimsuit. I was suddenly hyper-focused again and rushing to get out of my opening-number dress and into my swimsuit. Next came the butt glue—something we were *not* allowed on stage without. It's a strict MAO policy that all contestants use Sticky Hands, or what we contestants call "butt glue." Football players use it to help catch the ball, but in the pageant world, we use it to keep everything in place when we're walking on stage. The staff sprayed our behinds with it and then carefully sealed our bikini bottoms to our skin. I used my last few seconds to primp and then returned to the wing of the stage to wait for my turn.

I had been working my butt off—literally!—in the gym trying to get my body where I wanted it for this very moment. Nick Jonas was the music curator for the pageant, and he selected the song "Worth It" by Little Mix, which we all loved. I had rehearsed my walk so many times I could have done it in my sleep. I knew when and where I wanted my hands at all times, and I knew how and when I wanted to turn. I had my poses down, so when they called my name, I was ready. I flexed as hard as I could during my poses. I had put hours and hours into the gym, and it paid off; I felt strong and confident.

The swimsuit phase of the competition has faced harsh criticism for being outdated and shallow. Critics say this phase is judged solely on the physical appearances of the contestants and objectifies women. They say it pressures young girls into believing they must have perfect bodies in order to be Miss America. It's come under so much fire that MAO has since removed it from the competition altogether, and, to be quite honest, I disagree with this decision.

The swimsuit competition motivated me to start working out and eating healthier when I started doing pageants. It's not about how skinny or muscular you are; it's about having confidence and loving the skin you're in! I can't speak for everyone, of course, but I personally don't feel I should have to cover my body just because someone somewhere might (wrongly) objectify me.

My platform as Miss Georgia was "Healthy Children, Strong America." My parents are both physical therapists, and my dad's also a nutritionist. It only seemed natural that I took on that platform. From a young age, I understood the importance of taking care of my body, eating nutritious food, and exercising. I think it's important that we raise our children to understand these things so they, too, can lead healthy lifestyles. I wanted to encourage kids to put down the electronics, get outside, and play!

I love what both Vanessa Williams and Zendaya had to say about the swimsuit and evening gown phases when Brooke Burke asked them what they were looking for as judges.

"Confidence is the first thing," said Vanessa Williams. "From the first four steps, you can see their confidence and how they carry themselves."

And when Brooke asked Zendaya what she was looking for in the evening gown category, Zendaya answered, "It's confidence. It's poise...It's more than just makeup and hair. It's how you exude your confidence and how you feel inside."

To us as the contestants, it wasn't about strutting around on stage in a swimsuit, it was about working hard to care for our bodies and being confident in them!

Once all of us had walked for swimsuit, we lined up at the front of the stage and waved at the crowd. It was time for another commercial break, and the staff ran out and wrapped metallic, silver sarongs around our waists. When we came back, it was time to announce the top twelve. I felt way more confident about my evening gown and talent, so I was nervous about making it past swimsuit. I stood between Miss Iowa and Miss Florida.

"The first of the top twelve going on to compete for the crown is," Chris Harrison said, "Miss Florida, Mary Katherine Fechtel!" The crowd went wild. I hugged Mary Katherine, and she walked forward and waved at the crowd. Then they instructed her to hurry backstage to change for evening gown.

I was now standing between Miss Colorado and Miss Iowa, who were named as the second and third contenders in the top twelve.

More names were called, and I anxiously waited and prayed I would hear mine.

"Two more to announce," Chris said. "Congratulations, Miss Georgia, Betty Cantrell!" Relief flooded my body as I walked forward, waved to the crowd, and then hustled backstage to change into my gown.

Backstage, I was having the hardest time getting my evening gown on. It was the same gown Jay Reynolds had custom designed, which is a white two-piece. But my butt was so sticky from the glue that I couldn't pull my skirt up and over my hips.

"Does anybody have a wet wipe?" I asked desperately, but no one did. Thankfully, I managed to shimmy up my skirt. I even had enough time to put on my earrings and touch up my hair and makeup. For the first time that entire day, I felt relaxed. I had worn this gown at Miss Georgia, and I absolutely loved it. All I had to concentrate on was walking with poise and showing my confidence.

Walking in your evening gown is like your red-carpet moment. You want to walk at a slow and steady pace, soaking up the glamour. As I walked to "Fire and Gold" by Bea Miller, I looked out at the audience, and the weight of the whole experience sank in. I was filled with emotion and thinking how unbelievable it was for this to be happening. Then I tripped. Twice.

My skirt got tangled up in my feet, and I stuttered across the stage. *You've gotta be kidding me right now*, I thought, *I can't believe that just happened. Good grief, Betty. So stereotypical!* I saw the headlines about it already. I couldn't do anything about it, so I just shook my head and laughed. Then I looked toward the judges and saw them chuckling too.

After evening gown came the talent portion. All twelve of us went backstage and changed into our costumes. Mine was a red ball-gown with a fitted bodice and skirt and a billowing train. It was a dramatic gown for a dramatic piece. Then, we all returned to the stage, sat on a bench, and hoped our name would be called. The hosts named one contestant at a time, and if your name was called, that meant you made it into the top ten and would have the opportunity to perform. I sat on that bench and watched nine unique, strong performances. Three of us were left, but only one would advance.

As I watched the ninth performance, I thought, *Okay, this is it. Maybe I didn't make it.* I was devastated. If there was one thing I wanted out of this experience, it was to perform on national television. Chris Harrison paused before announcing the last contestant in the top ten: "Hey, Miss Georgia." I freaked out. I had been so stressed sitting there, and when I heard my name, I couldn't help but jump up a little. My dad said it looked like I had been "shot in the butt." As I headed to the center of the stage, I was smiling from ear to ear—so excited to perform, but I had to get into character since my aria was a dramatic piece.

As soon as I heard my music start, I felt a jolt of adrenaline. *Yes!* I thought, *Here I go! I'm doing this! Lord, please be with me.* I still wasn't feeling great after my sinus infection, but I wasn't even thinking about it. I just gave it all I had. As soon as I finished the last long, high note, I heard the crowd roar with applause. I could hear my dad's and Spencer's cheers above all the noise. I couldn't believe I had just performed on the Miss America stage! It definitely wasn't my best performance, but I was happy with it. And at least I hadn't tripped or lost an earring! I hurried off stage to change into my on-stage question outfit for the final phase of competition.

Of the ten of us who returned to the stage, only seven of us would have the opportunity to answer an on-stage question. When a contestant's name is called for this phase, she draws a slip of paper out of a bowl that has a judge's name on it. That judge then asks her a question. This is easily the most nerve-wracking part of the competition. You have twenty seconds to give an articulate response to a complicated, often controversial question in front of millions of people.

The first two girls' questions were political and what all of us expected and had prepared for. I prayed for a question like theirs. My name was called fifth, and I was both thrilled and terrified. I walked toward the silver bowl and drew Brett Eldredge's name. To no one's surprise, I was giddy to have drawn the name of a famous country music artist.

He started his question, and between his accent, the microphone, and the super loud crowd, I couldn't understand a single word he was saying. I wasn't ready for that. All I caught was something about Tom Brady.

"I'm sorry, can you repeat the question? I couldn't hear you. I'm sorry." I wasn't sure if I was even allowed to ask for the question to be repeated.

"New England Patriots quarterback, Tom Brady, was suspended for his part in the so-called Deflategate scandal then reinstated by the courts. Legalities aside, did Tom Brady cheat?"

"Did he cheat? Umm, that's a really good question." In my brain, I immediately thought, *Okay, this is a football question. I know nothing about this, so I'll make a joke about it.* "I'm not sure. I think I'd have to be there to see the ball and feel it and make sure it was deflated or not deflated."

I didn't hear any laughter from the crowd. They couldn't tell I had made a joke, and the crowd fell silent. I had to move on—quickly. But what could I say? If I said he did cheat, then all of New England would hate me. If I said he didn't, then the rest of the country would hate me. I decided to stay as neutral as possible while sticking to my personal principles: "But if there was a question there, then yes, I think he cheated. If there was any question to be had, I think that he definitely cheated and should have been suspended for that. That's not fair."

By the time I made it backstage, hot tears were rolling down my cheeks. *Really? A question about football!?* I thought. I barely knew who Tom Brady was, let alone cared about whether or not he cheated. I had lost for sure. Everyone else had received a political question, and their responses were strong and thoughtful. I tried to pull it together as I changed back into my evening gown for crowning. A bunch of the girls backstage tried to comfort me: "Betty, it's okay . . . you got a bad question . . . I don't know why they asked you that." I was touched by the sympathy and kindness of my fellow Miss America sisters, which made it even harder to regain my composure for the final part of the night.

The top seven returned to the stage. Miss America 2015, Kira Kizantsev, did her final walk as Miss America. Then Chris Harrison called us to the center of the stage. We stood in a line and held hands.

"The year started with more than eight thousand hopefuls competing in local competitions. Fifty-two, of course, made it to this stage in their state crowns. Now we're down to seven. Hard to believe. This card has five names: four runners up and the 2016 Miss America. When we've called the first runner-up, there will be three contestants left standing. One of them is your new Miss America, and I have the names right here. Are you ready?" Chris Harrison turned to face Brooke Burke.

Brooke took a moment to ask a few of the contestants for their thoughts. All of our stomachs were in knots. This was a weird, conflicting moment because part of you doesn't want your name called in hopes of being the winner, but part of you *does* want your name called as a runner-up because, of the girls in the final three, one is the winner and the other two place sixth and seventh and don't win a scholarship.

Chris started to announce the runners-up: "The fourth runner-up and the winner of an additional ten-thousand-dollar scholarship is...Miss Alabama, Meg McGuffin!"

Brooke continued: "The third runner-up to the 2016 Miss America and the winner of a fifteen-thousand-dollar scholarship is... Miss Louisiana, April Nelson!"

"The second runner-up gets an additional twenty-thousand-dollar scholarship, and she is...Miss Colorado, Kelley Johnson," Chris announced.

"One of you four ladies is the first runner-up to Miss America," Brooke explained. "You'll receive a twenty-five-thousand-dollar scholarship and will step into Miss America's shoes if she, for any reason, is unable to fulfill her duties. The 2016 Miss America first runner-up is...Miss Mississippi, Hannah Roberts!"

"We're down to the final three," Chris said.

I knew how much I had messed up that night. I lost my earring, stumbled during the evening gown, and totally blew my on-stage question. And I was standing next to two very, very strong girls who had done incredibly well throughout that entire week. There was no way I was going to win. For what felt like the hundredth time that night, I started to mentally prepare for the loss. Then, as the three of us stood there waiting, another one of my earrings fell off! I didn't want anyone to see that it had happened a second time, so I subtly stepped on it with my foot and dragged it under my dress.

Chris Harrison walked toward us and asked how we were doing. I confessed I had lost an earring during the competition twice now and laughed it off, trying to lighten the mood. Miss South Carolina and Miss Tennessee then shared what was running through their minds, and their responses were much more thoughtful than mine. We held each other as we waited for the announcement.

Chris started, "Your new Miss America is … Miss … Georgia!"

I couldn't believe my ears. *What? I won!?* I was truly surprised. *I'm Miss America?!* My emotions were all over the place as Kira placed the crown on my head, but mostly I was just so, so thankful. I couldn't have felt prouder of my state, and I was elated to be bringing the title home to them. Miss Georgia hadn't won in sixty-three years, and only one other Miss Georgia in the history of Miss America had won the title.

"Here she is! Your new Miss America," Chris said, "walking to the Bert Parks' classic, 'There She Is, Miss America!' Miss Georgia, the stage is yours. Take your walk down the runway!"

I hesitated at first, like a baby taking their first steps. I couldn't believe I was the one walking down the iconic, Miss America runway. I cradled my flowers and felt the crown on my head. I let the moment sink in as I started walking and waving at the crowd, still trying to make sense of what had just happened.

My mom and dad stood at the end of the runway in the crowd. Their divorce was final at this point, but it still wasn't comfortable for them to be together. Yet they had set their differences aside to come together to support and celebrate their daughter. It may seem like a small thing, but it was meaningful to me. I'll never forget that. I bent down and hugged them from the runway. Through tears, I thanked them and told them I loved them.

When I finished my first walk as Miss America and made it back to the stage, my class nearly tackled me with hugs. Every single one of those girls deserved to be Miss America. We were certainly all good enough, and I knew any one of them could have done just as good of a job as me—if not better. And despite popular belief, no one was ever mean or catty, at least not in my experience. People in the pageant world always say, "When you compete in Miss America, you meet your best friends and your future bridesmaids." At the time, I thought, *Yeah, sure, whatever. Doubt it.* But it's so true! Miss Wisconsin, Miss Missouri, and Miss Kansas were bridesmaids in my wedding. And our class of fifty-two still has a group chat, and we continue to text each other to this day.

Once the telecast was over, it was time for the press conference. I was escorted backstage and into a small room by the staff, and just like they promised, hair and makeup artists were there to touch me up. One dried my tears, put a new set of false eyelashes on me, and fixed my crown so it would stay in place. They even borrowed earrings from a fellow contestant since I was missing one. Cora with the Miss America Organization was also in the room and sat in a chair directly across from mine. She handed me three sheets of paper full of talking points for the press conference. Cora ran through everything I would need to say, including the people and sponsors I needed to thank.

Then Cora looked me square in the eye and asked, "Is there anything you need to tell me?"

Panic set in, and I forgot everything. I had been thinking about this moment for months now, ever since orientation when Cora warned us that she would be asking the winner this very question. My mom had reminded me to tell them about my unpaid speeding ticket, so I did: "Well, I do have a speeding ticket that I couldn't pay because I was here in Atlantic City instead of appearing at my court date."

"Okay, we'll get that taken care of," Cora assured me. "Don't worry about that."

"Other than that, I really don't think I have anything juicy to tell."

"Okay, are you sure?" She asked one more time.

"Yeah, I'm pretty sure. I've lived a very sheltered life, I promise."

I had roughly three minutes to study and memorize those papers. It was a firehose of information, and Cora must have sensed my stress.

"If you need help, look at me," she said. "I'll be in the corner, and I'll try to mouth what you need to say if you forget."

The staff guided me to the press conference room, and all of the celebrity judges and the judges from the prelims were there. As we waited for the press to be let into the room, I asked the judges, "How did this happen? Why did you pick me?"

They laughed and seemed to sense my surprise.

"You were the most real," Kevin O'Leary said. "We could all relate to you. All your little mishaps and mistakes, we've all been there, and that's who Miss America should be. She should be human; she should be relatable. And any little girl should be able to look up to Miss America and think, 'Oh, I could be Miss America because she's Miss America.'"

That made perfect sense to me, and I felt reassured to have won for being exactly myself. I also felt more confident and secure starting my new position as Miss America knowing Betty Cantrell was enough.

Then Brett Eldredge looked at me and said, "Betty, I am so sorry about that on-stage question. I did not write it; I just had to read it." I couldn't believe Brett Eldredge was apologizing to me! But it was also validating to hear he also thought it was a tricky question.

"That's okay, Brett," I smiled and nodded my head. "We can still be friends."

But on the inside, I was thinking, *Brett Eldredge is talking to me, and we're on a first-name basis!*

The doors opened, and the press and board members flooded into the room and practically stood shoulder to shoulder. Sam Haskell, who is now the former CEO and president of MAO, introduced me as the new Miss America. I waved and posed for a few photos before taking the podium. This was my first real moment as Miss America. A microphone loomed in front of me, and I suddenly had to be a public speaker. Even though I had studied theater, that material was always scripted. I'd never call myself a good public speaker, but when the time came for me to speak, I felt calm, and I know that was God's doing. I told myself, *You just won Miss America; you can do a press conference. You've got this.*

My brain took over, and I expressed gratitude for being crowned the new Miss America. I rattled off the sponsors and the other things I had mere minutes to memorize. I did look to Cora for a little bit of help when I was having trouble recalling a sponsor or two. Then someone from the press asked me about my on-stage question debacle.

"You know what?" I said. "I still don't know the answer to that question."

The people in the room laughed. Each of the judges was then given the opportunity to take the mic and elaborate on their reasons for choosing me. I was overwhelmed to hear each of them talk about my realness, relatability, and confidence, but most of all, I was overwhelmed by their reactions to my talent. They all said they were blown away by my opera performance. The judges are instructed not to show any facial expressions to avoid bias or favor, but Brett Eldredge admitted he couldn't help but tear up during my performance!

The press conference wrapped up, and I posed for pictures. Then it was straight to the after-party! I got to ride in a limo to the venue, which turned out to be party central. I was escorted through a side door, and as soon as they opened it, everyone inside started cheering! The area where I stood was roped off, and I felt like a celebrity. It was both strange and surreal; after all, I was just Betty from Georgia. Lights and balloons hung everywhere, and it was so crowded with people that there was hardly any space to move.

I looked out at the crowd, and just on the other side of the rope stood my Miss America sisters. They clapped for me, and it felt weird to be separated from them after having been with them all day, every day for the past two weeks. I walked to the center of the dance floor, and Sam Haskell introduced me to the crowd. He passed the microphone to me, and again I expressed my excitement and gratitude to be Miss America. I gestured toward the runners up who also stood on the dance floor, and again I stated that any one of my Miss America sisters could have been chosen and done an incredible job, and I was deeply grateful to represent them.

My family and Spencer were there too, and I got to hug them briefly before I was whisked away to greet a few notable people attending the party. If I were to guess, I'd say I spent a grand total of seven minutes at the after-party. But I understood that it isn't for the winner; it's for the contestants and the crowd to have fun and celebrate the night.

After my appearance at the after-party, I was brought back to the Taj Mahal hotel. On the night of her crowning, Miss America is awarded the suite on the top floor of whichever hotel she stayed at for the duration of the competition. She's also allowed twenty guests to celebrate with before wrapping up the night. As we walked through the lobby of the Taj Mahal, a huge entourage of people was guarding me, carrying the train of my dress, and holding my flowers. I was still wearing the crown, and the people we passed said things like, "That's the new Miss America!" and "She's from Georgia!" Again, it felt strange to be recognized and considered a celebrity, but it was also really cool.

I knew my family, Spencer, the Miss Georgia board, and the rest of my friends and family would be coming to my suite, so I was practically running to the elevator. With each floor that passed, my excitement grew. I entered the suite, and it was stunning—and bigger than any apartment I'd ever seen. It had two bedrooms, two bathrooms, a kitchen, a living room, and a dining room. It was practically a house!

Hors d'oeuvres had been set out, and a bartender stood ready to mix drinks. I think I ate two bites of something that I can't even remember; I was just too excited to eat. People from my list started coming in, and we were all on cloud nine. The Miss Georgia board was over the moon with excitement. I remember holding hands with them and jumping up and down as they kept saying, "You're Miss America! You did it!"

All my favorite people were together to celebrate this unbelievable night with me. My parents, Mikey, Sophia, and Spencer were there, of course. My aunts and uncles came too. My best friend from high school, Savanna, was even there. Natalie had been able to attend the prelims, but she had to return home for ballet rehearsals, so her mom came in Natalie's place. It was such a happy night.

After thirty minutes, the MAO staff started to wind down the party: "Alright. It's been thirty minutes. Time to go, everyone." Anyone who wasn't family had to leave, including Spencer. We stepped into the bedroom for a sliver of privacy as we said goodbye, but we kept the doors open.

Spencer took me by the hands, looked me in the eyes, and said, "I'm going to be here for you throughout this whole year. Your life is about to change, and I'm going to be here waiting for you when you're done."

I started crying. The night had been an emotional roller coaster, and I didn't want him to leave. He had been by my side throughout this entire experience and had been such a comfort to me. As we stood face to face and held hands, someone took a beautiful picture of us, and I've since had it printed on a canvas and hung in our house. I love that photo because it reminds me of our commitment to be there for each other no matter what.

I hung out with family for a while longer, and it was such a welcome break from the chaos of the evening. My aunts and uncles left, then Mikey and Sophia, and finally my dad. That entire day had been a whirlwind, and I was grateful to have had time with my family.

Then it was just my mom and me. Earlier that week, she had attended a parent meeting where she was told she would need to pack my bags for my year as Miss America. I was permitted two suitcases for the entire year, and my mom would have to take the rest of my things back home with her. Thankfully, my bags were already in the suite. The hostesses had told the contestants the night before finals to pack all of our things in case we won; that way, our bags would be waiting for us in the winner's suite.

My mom started going through everything and packing only what I would need. I had a full day of interviews and meetings the next morning. So while she graciously packed my things, I knew I needed to get whatever little sleep I could. I think it was four in the morning when I finally crawled into bed, and it was then that I realized I was still wearing the crown. I reluctantly pulled it off my head and set it on the nightstand. Then I closed my eyes and fell asleep.

***

Kacey Musgraves sings a song I absolutely love called "Pageant Material." It's all about how she *isn't* pageant material. It's a funny song, and at the end she sings, "I would rather lose for what I am than win for what I ain't." That resonates so deeply with me because even though I technically am a pageant girl now, no one would have ever labeled me—a farm girl who grew up in a double-wide trailer —as one.

I didn't win Miss America for being perfect or pretending to be someone who was. I won Miss America for being true to myself— mistakes, mishaps, and all. I was 100 percent Betty Cantrell as I picked off fake fingernails, tripped, lost earrings, talked about lost earrings, poorly answered a question about Tom Brady, and generally messed up a lot. It's just who I am. Spencer will tell you I can't even get through a meal without spilling something. In fact, my whole family uses a phrase whenever someone has some kind of mishap; they say someone "pulled a Betty," and they're not wrong!

It made me so proud to be a role model for every little girl out there who feels like she can't be herself *and* be Miss America. The truth is that you *can* be yourself, and I'm living proof of that. It doesn't matter who you are or where you came from. Miss America is not a mold that only one type of girl fits into; Miss America is a shape-shifter. Miss America is whoever takes on that role, and she can be anybody—whether that's a girl who's done pageants all her life or a girl who grew up on a farm in rural Georgia. I was exactly who God made me to be, and that was good enough to be Miss America.

CHAPTER 9

A Year Wearing the Crown

After forty-five brief but blissful minutes of sleep, I woke up to my first full day as Miss America. It took a minute for my new reality to sink in, and then my chest tightened. This was a completely new role to me and yet one of the greatest things to have ever happened in my life. I felt the weight of the expectations and desperately wanted to perform my new role perfectly.

That morning, a driver picked me up from the Taj Mahal and took me back to Boardwalk Hall where I had been crowned the night before. It was time to get ready for my first activity as Miss America: the infamous "toe dip." This is a tradition where Miss America walks down the boardwalk to the beach and dips her toes into the Atlantic Ocean. It sounds idyllic and straight out of a music video, but it looks more like someone running through the water and splashing around like a kid while the press takes pictures.

By this point, I was still so, so exhausted from the last two weeks and running on fumes. So when I saw that the same hair and makeup artists who fixed me up after I won the night before were already at Boardwalk Hall to help get me ready, I was overcome with feelings of relief and gratitude. Once I was dressed and my crown was in place, I walked—surrounded by MAO staff and security—to the beach. The press, my family, and Spencer were already gathered there. When I stepped into the water, goosebumps covered my body, but I was so focused on doing a good job that I hardly noticed how cold I felt. I was trying to run through the waves as least awkwardly as possible. I did my best to look at the camera, smile, and pose without getting knocked over. Everyone's eyes were on me, and I could feel them.

After the toe dip, we began walking back to Boardwalk Hall and passed the famous Miss America statue that stands right outside the building. The bronze beauty queen wears a gown, sash, and crown and holds a crown out in front of her as if to crown the next Miss America. The MAO staff told me to stop at the statue and gesture to it as the new Miss America while a photographer took photos.

Atlantic City has always been the home of the Miss America pageant, so the locals are some of Miss America's biggest fans. People started coming up to me and asking to take pictures together. I took photos with some sweet little girls. The way they looked up at me wearing the crown—their expressions a mixture of fascination and awe—made my new reality as Miss America sink in. It was the perfect start to my year.

We returned to the Taj Mahal for my suitcases, and it was time to say goodbye to my family and Spencer. I didn't know when I would see them next. My year-long tour was about to start, and New York City was my first stop. My first two and a half months of the tour were media appearances, which meant countless interviews and events, and I'd be traveling the entire year with my tour managers, Alice and Liz, who were total strangers to me at this point. I hugged my family members and said goodbye, and when I got to Spencer, I couldn't stop myself from sobbing. Spencer, also teary-eyed, lowered his sunglasses over his eyes.

"Alright, we really need to go," Alice said apologetically. Spencer and I hugged one last time, and then I made my way to the limo. As I looked back at Spencer, I noticed he was looking down, and my heart felt like it was being torn into pieces. I climbed into the limo where Alice, Cora, and a public relations staff member were already seated. I had just bawled my eyes out in front of them. I don't love showing my emotions in front of people, let alone people I barely know. I tried to collect myself. I wiped my tears and thought, *Alright Betty, get it together.*

The drive from Atlantic City to New York was a long one—long enough for me to do five or six phone interviews on the way there. Cora and Alice coached me on talking points, telling me what to say, what not to say, and what to focus on. It was dark when we arrived at our hotel that night, and I was completely worn out from the lack of sleep.

Before I went to my room, Cora said, "Tomorrow morning, you're going to be on *Good Morning America*. You need to be ready to go by 4:00 a.m."

"Yes, ma'am," I answered.

When I got to my room that night, I was finally alone for the first time. *Whoa! What is happening*, I thought. It felt strange, and the entirety of the experience was catching up to me. I sat on the bed and let myself cry. I needed to let it all out—every emotion I'd felt from the last two weeks. Then I called my mom, dad, and Spencer to let them know I had arrived safely to New York before passing out.

I woke up at 3:00 a.m. the following morning to get ready for my first televised interview. Most of the interviews for the next two months started with the same question: "Betty, you were just crowned Miss America, how does it feel?"

At first, it was easy to express my excitement and gratitude: "It's amazing! I get to wear a crown to work every day. I am just so thankful to represent such an incredible group of young women. I feel so humbled by this opportunity and cannot wait to see what this year has in store." But after two months of interview after interview after interview, the rush of having won was no longer new. I feared my responses sounded stale and insincere, but I did my best to relive how it had felt to win.

Once the first couple months of media appearances were behind me, I was able to focus on service work. One of my favorite aspects of the job was serving as a National Goodwill Ambassador for Children's Miracle Network Hospitals. I visited their hospitals all across the country on an almost weekly basis. I'd visit room by room, so the kids and I would have quality, one-on-one time together. We'd sing songs, color, read books, talk, and just hang out. They loved seeing Miss America, and I genuinely loved seeing them.

My time with the Miracle Kids and their families was one of the greatest joys and honors of my entire year. The bonds I made with them have endured, and I still talk to many of the families. It was powerful, humbling work and especially meaningful to me because I have loved kids ever since I was a little girl. My mom loves to tell a story of when I was four years old, and all I wanted for Christmas was a purple book with pictures of babies in it. She somehow found one, and when

I opened it, I excitedly flipped through the pages. I carried that book around until the spine was falling apart.

As Miss America, I got to do glamorous things too, like attend red carpet events and award shows. Those were my favorite! I even got to present awards at the Country Music Awards, the American Music Awards, the Academy of Country Music Awards, and the Billboard Music Awards. My first award show was the forty-ninth annual CMAs, and I was scheduled to present "Song of the Year" alongside Darius Rucker. When we arrived, I stepped out of a black, tinted-window Suburban wearing the crown and a stunning, beaded Sherri Hill gown the organization had sent for me to wear. It was a little too big, but it was impossible to feel anything short of amazing in it. The crowd cheered, and I heard people saying, "That's Miss America!" I felt like royalty!

I posed on the red carpet while photographers took pictures. Then, when the photos were posted online, the anonymous chat boards exploded with criticism of my appearance. People were calling me fat and writing how I had already gained weight because of the size of my dress and how it looked on me. I'd been cyberbullied before, but this was my first red-carpet appearance as Miss America, and the criticism stung.

Then, just a few weeks later, I was scheduled to present at the American Music Awards with Kevin O'Leary, one of the celebrity judges from the Miss America pageant. The organization made sure I did *not* wear my crown at any more red-carpet events. It turned out I wasn't supposed to wear it at the CMAs either, but we somehow hadn't received that memo beforehand.

Side note: I never understood the no-crown policy for red-carpet events. The crown was my dead giveaway and naturally attracted the press. And without it, events were a little awkward for me. Fans scream and freak out over the celebrities, but whenever I stepped out without the crown, people just stared at me, puzzled. They had no idea who I was. Celebrities raised their eyebrows at me, and their expressions said, "Who is this girl on our red carpet?" Or they'd straight up ask me who I was, and when I explained that I was Miss America, their next question was inevitably, "So where's your crown?" It was humbling to say the least.

I was waiting in a green room until it was time for Kevin O' Leary and me to appear on stage when Liz said, "Oh, look! There's Harrison Ford."

"What?!" I gasped. My heart started racing, and my eyes searched the room for him. Harrison Ford is easily one of the most famous, handsome, coolest actors of all time. He's Han Solo for goodness' sake! He's Indiana Jones!

"Yeah," Liz confirmed. "He's right there!"

Sure enough, Harrison Ford was fewer than ten feet away from me. A new *Star Wars* film was set to release soon, so he was attending the AMAs to promote it.

I wasn't wearing my crown and felt too embarrassed to approach him. My excitement and apprehension literally made my eyes water.

"Oh my gosh, Liz. Do you think it's possible for me to get a picture with him?"

"Yeah. Just go ask him."

But he was rehearsing his lines. *Ugh*, I thought, *I won't bother him.* I decided to patiently wait until I could see he was done rehearsing, and then I'd walk over to him and politely ask. But as soon as he was finished, his management escorted him away. I'd missed my opportunity. *Nooo!* I groaned inside my head.

Five minutes later, Liz said, "Look, he's back!"

This time, I walked right up to him and tapped him on the shoulder.

"Mr. Harrison Ford," I said (I had no idea what to call him). "Excuse me. Hi. I'm Betty. I'm Miss America 2016, and I would love to get a picture with you." I was shamelessly fangirling but also trying to play it cool and not weird him out.

"Oh, sure," he said.

We took only one picture; there was no way I was going to ask for two.

"So you're Miss America?" he asked.

"Yes sir!"

"That's so cool."

Harrison Ford said I was cool! Then he walked toward the door, looked over his shoulder, and said, "Hey, thanks for the picture."

Shaking, I walked back over to Liz. We had a miniature celebration over what had just happened, and that was easily one of the highlights of my year as Miss America.

Christmas rolled around, and I was itching to do something big and different—something no other Miss America had done. I only had one year in this role, and I wanted to do something personal that would also have an impact.

I told Spencer about what I wanted to do over Facetime one night: "I think I'm going to cut my hair." I was a little worried about what he would think.

"Do it!" he said without hesitation.

"No. When I say cut it, I mean I want to chop it all off."

"Yeah! Do it!" Spencer's always down for crazy and spontaneous.

I had always loved hearing stories about Locks of Love, a nonprofit organization benefiting kids with long-term hair loss. Donors grow their hair long, then cut it and donate it to the organization, which turns the donated hair into hair pieces for children. It's a beautiful organization with a big heart, and I wanted to be part of their story.

In the pageant world, I was kind of known for my long, thick hair. Many girls in pageant competitions use hair extensions, but I didn't need to thanks to my Greek genes. And once I won Miss America, there were even fan pages dedicated to my hair, which I found both flattering and hilarious—if not a little ridiculous. Since my hair literally had a reputation of its own, I thought it would be that much more meaningful to donate it to Locks of Love. I hoped it would turn the stereotype of pageant girls and their big hair on its head and make a positive statement. And more importantly, I didn't need my hair. I could always grow it back, and I would rather donate it to someone who *did* need it.

But first, I had to get it approved by the MAO board. They were reluctant at first and worried it might not look good.

"I really want to do this," I said. "I don't care if it doesn't look good."

The board wanted to turn it into a big marketing/PR stunt and suggested having me appear on *Ellen*. As much as I would have loved to meet Ellen DeGeneres (I mean, who wouldn't?!), it didn't feel right under those circumstances.

"I'm not totally comfortable with that," I pushed back. "I don't want to make it a big thing. I just want to do it on my own, as a personal thing."

"Okay," the board finally agreed. "If you really, really want to."

I had a one-week break coming up for Christmas, which was going to be my first time back home since winning the title, so I planned to visit my hairdresser in Warner Robins. When I showed her a picture of a pixie cut, she explained how my hair was too thick and would stick out all over the place. It wouldn't be cute, and I'd hate it, she warned me. So together, we found a short hairstyle that would work and ended up cutting off more than twelve inches. As soon as she brushed the stray hairs off my shoulders, I posted a photo of my new look on social media.

It turned out that cutting my hair was a much bigger deal than I had anticipated. I took a lot of heat for it. According to haters on social media, my hair looked hideous, and I was so much prettier with long hair. They also criticized me for the organization I chose and said I should have donated it to Pantene Beautiful Lengths instead because Pantene was a better charity. The criticism stunned me. Who knew there was a wrong way to donate your hair? I had to frequently remind myself not to let it affect me. I didn't cut my hair as a publicity stunt, and I didn't do it for self-gratification. I wanted to do a good thing, and there hasn't been a single day that I've regretted having done it. I'd do it all over again.

With the turn of the year came the United Service Organization (USO) tour, which was absolutely incredible. It used to be that every Miss America did a USO tour back in the day, but it's actually pretty rare now. I was desperately hoping I would get to do one, and when I found out that I would, in fact, have the opportunity, I couldn't share the news with anyone because it was considered top secret information and could pose a security risk. I, of course, thought it was the coolest thing ever to be a part of something that was top secret!

On the tour were the vice chairman of the joint chiefs of staff as well as celebrities like country music singer Craig Morgan, UFC fighters Cowboy Cerrone and Anthony Pettis, and Charles Tillman

from the Carolina Panthers. I was to host the USO show and introduce the other celebrities on the tour. I'd also get to perform a few
songs myself.

We traveled through seven countries in eight days, starting in
Alaska, then flying to Okinawa, Crete, Baghdad, Kuwait, Thailand,
Portugal, and then back to Washington D.C. It was scary at times,
especially in Baghdad and Kuwait, which were active war zones.
Everyone on those bases was armed and ready for action. I even
found out after we left Kuwait that a bomb had gone off on one of the
roads that we had come in on, which was why we had to exit using
a different route. It was a tremendous honor to spend so many days
with these people and to perform for the men and women who literally put their lives on the line for our freedom every single day. It was
an experience I will never forget.

One of my major goals during my time as Miss America was
to make professional connections for my singing career. I was given
incredible opportunities to perform at large venues and with huge
symphony orchestras across the nation. I loved it, and it's how I met
my music producer, Steve Ivey. On the day I met him, I was attending
a donor event in Savannah, Georgia, for Mercer University. I spoke to
the audience and sang "Georgia on My Mind."

Afterward, Steve approached me and introduced himself and his wife, Sandy. He was an alumni board member at
Mercer and told me how impressed he was with my voice. Then he
asked, "When can you come to Nashville and record an album?"
I felt like I was going to burst with excitement. This was huge! It was
the moment I'd been working toward my whole life!

I called Spencer as soon as I got back to my hotel room. He was
just as elated as I was, and we immediately began to plan how and

when we would visit Nashville to meet with Steve. It turned out I had an upcoming event in Nashville, so Spencer met me there, and together, we met with Steve after I wrapped up my Miss America events for the day. Steve wanted to start working on an album as soon as my year as Miss America was over. He and Spencer exchanged contact information and made plans to stay in touch for when the time came. I had set my dream of launching a singing career into motion!

About two and a half months before my reign as Miss America came to an end, I was in New York City with my tour manager, Alice. We had a press interview scheduled over lunch, which was unusually casual, but I figured it was with a friend of the organization or something. I didn't think much of it. I wasn't told who the journalist was or which publication she was writing for, but that wasn't out of the ordinary. These kinds of details often weren't shared with me. I was simply expected to show up and do my thing.

Alice and I arrived at the restaurant and met up with the journalist and Jessica, a public relations representative from Dick Clarke Productions, the company that puts on the pageant every year for American Broadcasting Company (ABC). The journalist was a young woman—I would guess somewhere in her early twenties.

The restaurant was upscale, and the menu was fancier and trendier than what I was used to. I couldn't pronounce any of the entrées, and I was unfamiliar with half of the ingredients in the dish descriptions. When the server came to take our order, I jokingly asked if they had anything normal to eat. Alice laughed. She was plenty familiar with my sense of humor by now. I decided on a rotisserie chicken sandwich.

The journalist pulled out a recording device, which surprised me, but neither Alice nor Jessica objected, so I didn't say anything.

At first, her questions for me were very casual—the getting-to-know-you type. Then she asked me what the hardest part about being Miss America was. Now, it probably comes as no surprise that I'm terrible at holding my tongue. I've always been someone who says it like it is, especially if I feel like more needs to be said or if I'm being mistreated.

"I guess parades are the worst thing," I admitted. I went on to explain how my duties were limited to standing and waving during parades, but I'd rather be out in the crowd and interacting with people. To me, today's modern Miss America can and should do more than stand, wave, and look pretty.

Then the questions turned more political. She asked about the upcoming presidential election and other current controversial topics. A few times, Alice and Jessica interjected before I could answer and told me, "Don't answer that," which was both frustrating and a relief. Few political opinions are universally popular, so having an out from some of the questions was helpful. But at the same time, MAO is an organization that prides itself on empowering women and amplifying our voices. We're asked political questions during the pageant and expected to have informed opinions, so why not share them? It seemed contradictory to me to be prohibited from speaking my mind.

The journalist then asked questions that were more personal: Did I have a boyfriend? Did I miss him? Was it hard being separated for a year? I was happy to talk about something lighthearted and personal, and I gave her my honest answers. The journalist and I were close in age, and the interview began to feel like a casual conversation over lunch with a girlfriend.

The interview lasted a good hour while we ate. I answered the questions as honestly as I could when allowed. As we wrapped up, the journalist told me she was going to attend the next Miss America pageant to see me pass off the crown and expressed how excited she was to meet Spencer. I thanked her and said I looked forward to reading the article. I thought it went well and hoped it would be a good outgoing interview as one of my last as Miss America.

The article came out two weeks later titled "'Parades Are the Worst': Miss America Reflects on Her Reign." I felt like someone had punched me in the gut. Needless to say, it could not have been a less favorable article. I had been villainized to sound like a high-maintenance, self-absorbed brat with terrible table manners. All my words had been twisted and taken out of context. This journalist, who I mistakenly trusted, took everything I said and spun it negatively. She even criticized how I ate my lunch and asked the waiter for help.

I know this happens all the time in journalism, and it shouldn't be a big deal, but this article blew up in the pageant world. Everyone was talking about it. People were bashing me on chat boards, saying things like, "I knew she was the worst Miss America. This just confirms it," "I hate her," and "I'll never let my daughter look up to someone who's so ungrateful to be Miss America." I was devastated.

At the time it was published, I was in a small town in Pennsylvania for an event. I Facetimed Spencer from my hotel room and bawled my eyes out. It felt like the entire world hated me, and there was nothing Spencer could say to comfort me because he knew that I was kind of right. I had to get on a conference call almost immediately with the CEO, CFO, and other leaders in the organization. I knew they were angry. Rather than say, "Betty, you've done five hundred interviews this year, and this is the first negative one. That seems weird," the MAO leadership sarcastically apologized for not realizing how much I hated being Miss America.

Their response, of course, made me cry even harder. I tried so hard to go above and beyond what was required of my role as Miss America throughout that entire year. I wanted nothing more than to represent everyone well—my class, the organization, my state, my family, and myself.

"You have to know that I didn't say those things like that," I pleaded. "Alice and Jessica were sitting there. Do you really think they would have let me talk like that to a journalist?"

We discussed the article at length, and I felt like they started to understand what happened from my perspective and believe me to some extent. That article deeply hurt me and the organization. Everyone involved looked bad. Jessica was fired, and Alice was nearly fired. I was terrified and wracked with guilt. I was also sent home as a punishment. The appearances and events that had been booked for that week were canceled. It was mortifying, and people were talking about how the organization would strip me of my crown like they had done to other "badly behaved" former Miss Americas.

I wanted to issue an apology on social media and explain my perspective, but the organization forbid me from posting anything. They didn't want me to talk about it. I felt completely powerless over my own reputation—a reputation I worked hard to earn. The whole debacle sent me into a deep depression, and it was easily the lowest point during my year.

The truth is that there are some not-so-great parts about being Miss America. As with any job, it has its challenges. I tried to share this information with the incoming class of the 2017 Miss America contestants and their state directors during their orientation, but the board only gave me ten minutes to speak to them. When I attended orientation as a contestant, I remember wanting to hear the *real* stuff from Miss America 2015, Kira Kizantsev, so I wanted to do the same for the new class. I felt they deserved to hear a realistic account of what to expect from the job they were all competing for. I was not given the opportunity then, but this book is my chance to share what the life of Miss America *really* looks (or looked) like.

Each month, I traveled roughly twenty thousand miles and lived in hotels. A lot of people think that Miss America gets an apartment in New York City like Miss USA does, but that's not the case. As Miss America, you're at the airport every two days—flying to your next destination, checking into your next hotel, and eating your next room-service meal . . . alone. It may sound glamorous—and in some ways it is—but it also gets lonely. I missed sharing meals with my friends and family, and I missed having one place to come home to.

The workload was also intense. Miss Americas who sing generally end up performing twice as much as Miss Americas with other kinds of talent. For example, a Miss America who danced as her talent would usually give a speech and then do a meet and greet. But as a singing Miss America, I would give a speech, perform two songs, and finish with a meet and greet. I was performing nearly every day and often more than once.

Even though the Miss America contract states that your appearances as the titleholder shouldn't exceed four hours, most of my appearances lasted much longer. In fact, twelve-hour days were a regular occurrence whenever I appeared and performed at multiple events in one day. There was always something—some phone call I had to be on, some interview, some conference call with the organization, something I had to be ready for. I always had to be "on" and camera ready. And unless it was a major red-carpet event, my hair and makeup were my responsibilities. I got very little rest or sleep. It was tough and left me extra, extra tired.

I also had very little control—even over the more mundane aspects of my life. I lived out of two suitcases and didn't get to pick what clothes I wore. I had to wear whatever was sent to me, and it didn't matter whether I liked it or if it even fit. At one point, my tour managers shared a memo with me that some of the board members sent, which said I should no longer wear pants at events—only skirts and dresses. I was shocked and wouldn't stand for it, so I called Sam, the CEO at the time, and expressed my concerns: "This is 2016! As a woman, I should be allowed to wear pants. Many of the clothing items sent to me from the sponsor *are* pants!" Thankfully, he concurred and overruled the board.

A lot of people think all of Miss America's expenses are covered by the organization, but that's not the case. I didn't have a shoe or jewelry sponsor, so I was financially responsible for those things. I also had no hair or makeup sponsor, which meant I had to pay for all of my beauty products. I was in full hair and makeup nearly every day; that's a *lot* of hair and makeup products! I begged the board to provide a beauty stipend of some sort not only for me but also for all future Miss Americas. They agreed to issue a $1,200 stipend for my year, but I had to fight for it.

My social media accounts were monitored and run by MAO too. Whereas Miss USA is allowed to have her personal Instagram account and her Miss USA account, I had to give MAO all of my social media usernames and passwords. They then deactivated my accounts when I was crowned and would sometimes make posts on my behalf and write captions in my voice without my permission, as if I had made the post myself. I had virtually no control over my social media presence and was prohibited from sharing anything about my real life.

The pressure of having to wake up every morning and look the part of Miss America, whose image is one of beauty and perfection, was more pressure than I can describe. Not only was I worried about falling short of the general public's expectations of how I should look, but I was also worried about disappointing the organization. I was sometimes told things like, "You need to go back and put more makeup on," and "You need to go back and change clothes." If I looked bad (or good) in a picture posted on social media, the anonymous chat boards were always full of criticism: "Oh, man, she is the sloppiest Miss America," and "Did you see her hair today?" It got to a point where I dreaded seeing my name mentioned on social media because I knew if I didn't look perfect, happy, and put together every single day, then someone was going to have something to say about it.

Of all the challenges that came with the role of Miss America, the relentless cyberbullying was by far the hardest. I was thrust into the spotlight, and the things people said were so hurtful it astounded me:

> "Betty is so beautiful. I love her until she speaks."

> "Better get back in school, Betty. Maybe you can be a music teacher. Nobody outside of the area where you live is going to pay to see you."

> "Please, half of Betty's appearances while she was Miss America for the year were in Georgia. She was home with the boyfriend. Ha ha."

> "Betty is the worst Miss America of this century."

"My guess is that within a year, Betty will be pregnant and back in Georgia. It is so sad that what should have been a great year for Georgia turned out to be a nightmare."

"I think she was just too immature to handle the job of being Miss America and understand what was important."

It felt like everyone had something to say about me, and yet no one actually knew me or had any idea what it was like to be Miss America. No one knew what I was going through. But the haters were always there like vultures, ready to tear me apart. I struggled with cyberbullying as Miss America, and I still struggle with it now.

It hurts me to know there are people out there who don't like me, who want to see me fail, and who think that I was a terrible Miss America. That's truly, truly painful. It gnaws at me. It reminds me of an episode of *The Office*, my favorite TV show, where Pam says, "I even hate that Al-Qaeda hates me. I think if they got to know me, they wouldn't hate me." That's exactly how I feel about cyberbullies, and it's not an ego thing. I don't *need* people to love me, but I'm a people pleaser. I want to make people happy, and I want to be liked—like most every other human being.

Fame is a double-edged sword. Yes, it's fun to have a lot of followers on social media, but I've also learned that with it comes tremendous negativity. I think it's easy for people to forget that public figures and celebrities are real people with real feelings. Unkind words hurt me just like they hurt you. We're all human beings—we all have souls and feelings, and we all long to be accepted.

It took me forever to understand that you can't control what other people think or say about you; you can only control you. Instead of taking what people say to heart or engaging in the meanness, you have to let it go and focus on making yourself a better, more gracious, more forgiving person. As difficult as it is, you have to pray for those people. You can't let them get to you. You have to grow a thick skin to get through this thing called life, especially in today's world of social media.

I had days where I felt like I couldn't do it anymore. The travel, the exhaustion, the pressure, the lack of control, and the cyberbullying were overwhelming. I was hurting, and I wanted to go home. Every city meant one more hotel room with no one in it but me. At the same time though, I recognized I had signed up for this job. The fact that this was an enormous privilege and opportunity that so many women would love to experience was anything but lost on me. It was a total paradox. And I could see both the good and the bad from my perspective.

And there truly was so much good that happened that year. One of the most upsetting things about the negative article released about me was that the journalist conveniently failed to mention the tons of amazing things I told her about being Miss America. Yes, I was exhausted and overwhelmed at times, and yes, I missed my boyfriend and my family. But I was performing for huge crowds like I had *always* dreamed. I was even asked to sing during the live telecast of the Miss America 2017 pageant. It had been years since a Miss America had done that, and I still have no words for my gratitude for having been given that opportunity.

I had the great privilege of serving communities and people I genuinely cared about. I performed for our beloved men and women in uniform on the USO tour. I laid a wreath at the tomb of the unknown soldier during a beautiful ceremony. I sang the national anthem for mothers of fallen, active-duty soldiers who MAO crowns as honorary Miss Americas. My performance for them may not have been my best because I cried throughout the entire thing. I was incredibly moved and honored to be a part of something so meaningful.

And I was given opportunities that completely blew me away. I traveled to places some people may never have the resources to visit. I even toured the White House! I may not have met the now former president Barack Obama, but I *did* get to meet his dogs, which is still pretty cool if you ask me! I was making professional and personal connections that were and still are invaluable to me.

As Miss America, I felt like I was truly making a difference in the world. Any shortcomings that came with the job didn't matter at the end of the day. The time I spent giving motivational speeches at high schools, inspiring young people to be themselves and follow their dreams, and putting smiles on the faces of Miracle Kids with that crown on my head was so gratifying that it made the toughest parts of being Miss America totally worth it.

My year as Miss America was without a doubt the toughest year of my life to date, and I wouldn't trade it for anything. I am honored and blessed to have been Miss America 2016. My time in that role helped me grow as a person and in ways I never could have anticipated. Even my relationship with God grew stronger. I prayed constantly that year, mostly for strength and patience, and I learned to depend on him in ways I had never done before.

You will experience times in your life when things seem impossible—times when everything feels like it's falling apart, and you don't know up from down. But you can trust in God, knowing that everything you are doing right now is preparation for what's next. All the little things you've done and continue to do are God's way of preparing you for what he has planned for your future. The time I spent memorizing lines for *The Wizard of Oz* prepared me for the moment when I was given five minutes to memorize a sheet of talking points for my first major press conference. You may not be able to see it now, but God is always readying you. Trust that he is in control.

When the time came to pass on the crown to Miss America 2017 on the Boardwalk Hall stage, I was ready. But in true Betty fashion, I messed up again. At the end of the ceremony, I had been carefully holding the sash so that when I placed it over the winner, the lettering would be facing out and not upside down. But when Savvy Shields was named the new Miss America, I walked toward her and instinctually gave her a hug. During our hug, the sash somehow turned inside out, and I didn't realize it until I was placing it over Savvy.

"It's backwards!" I said as I pulled it back from her. She started laughing and was so gracious about my final blunder as Miss America. "I'm so sorry," I said as I pinned the coveted crown on her head. I wouldn't be Betty if I didn't mess up in some shape or fashion. I was embarrassed, but at that point I didn't care.

Savvy took her first walk like I had done one year ago, and I stood there crying, laughing, and clapping. I probably looked like a lunatic, but I was overcome with so many emotions: joy for Savvy, relief for myself, gratitude for the whole experience, and excitement for the next chapter of my life.

I was ready to go home, rest, and be myself again—just Betty Cantrell, not Miss America 2016. Every outgoing Miss America I've ever talked to has said she felt that same way too. It had been a long, wonderful, and exhausting year. And as excited as I had been to begin my reign as Miss America, I was just as excited for the year to come to an end. I was finally going home to my family and Spencer. And what no one knew during that crowning ceremony was that I had so much to look forward to.

CHAPTER 10

Find Yourself a Spencer

As soon as the Miss America 2017 telecast was over, I bolted to my dressing room. Beforehand, I had talked to Liz, my tour manager: "When I come back from crowning the new Miss America, can I please have my mom and Spencer waiting in my dressing room?"

"I'm on it." Liz and I had grown incredibly close during my year, and I trusted she would make it happen.

The MAO does not allow Miss America to mention her romantic life because they want her to be known as America's sweetheart. I think this image is dated and unrealistic, especially since most every girl I competed with was either already engaged or soon to be. Regardless, the policy meant I had to keep my relationship with Spencer under wraps throughout my entire year as Miss America— no social media posts, no mentioning him in interviews, and certainly no public displays of affection. Not even handholding. But now that I had passed on the crown, all those rules were lifted.

I opened the door, and when I saw Spencer, my eyes filled with tears. I was so happy to be near him without a watchful eye. We immediately embraced and kept saying how much we missed each other.

"Am I allowed to post something?" I asked Alice.

"You're not Miss America anymore," Alice smiled. "You can do whatever you want."

Over the past year, I had taken thousands of photos of my travels and events, and all I wanted to do now was post a photo of Spinny and me. And I knew exactly which picture I wanted to share: it was from the night before the 2017 Miss America telecast.

On the eve of the telecast, my mom offered to take a few pictures of Spencer and me.

"Wait!" I said. I excitedly reached into my purse for a tiny, white box. I opened it up, pulled out my engagement ring, and slid it on my finger. That's right; Spencer and I were already engaged!

Contrary to the popularly held belief among my haters who said I spent all my time as Miss America in Georgia with my boyfriend, I only saw Spencer a handful of times throughout my year. We talked on the phone and had Facetime calls all the time, but I only saw him in person the few times I happened to be in Georgia, once in Nashville, and once in Florida. He'd meet me in whatever city I was staying, and we'd have dinner together before having to say goodbye. The distance was incredibly hard, but breaking up was never a topic of discussion. Neither of us ever said, "This doesn't make sense" or "I can't do this anymore." We were committed to making it work from the beginning.

In early August, about a month before I passed on the crown, I had three empty days on my calendar, so I begged the board for some vacation time. Spencer and his family were going to be in Siesta Key, Florida, on those very same days, and I would be wrapping up the Miss America Outstanding Teen Pageant just two hours away in Orlando. The board granted its permission, and I started counting down the days until I could see Spencer!

On my first day of vacation, I woke up at 6:00 a.m. to get on the road to Siesta Key as early as possible. Even though I was worn out from the MAO Teen events from the past week, I couldn't wait to get to the beach and relax with my man! Spencer had warned me ahead of time that we were going on a brunch cruise with his parents as soon as I arrived, so I made sure my hair and makeup were done before I got there. As I pulled into the parking lot of the condo, it started drizzling. And then I saw Spencer standing on the sidewalk in a white button-down shirt, holding an umbrella. *Of course*, I thought. *Always the gentleman.*

He helped me out of the car, grabbed my bags, and thanked the driver. Then he opened the trunk of his parents' car and put my bags inside.

"Why aren't we taking them to the room?" I asked, confused.

"We're late. We've got to meet my parents. They're already on the boat."

We started walking down a cement pathway that led around the condo and toward the beach, which was empty at that hour. Giant palm trees towered over us. We had the whole place to ourselves, and it was beautiful. Then Spencer suddenly slowed his pace. *I thought we were in a hurry?* I wondered.

Elvis Presley's "I Can't Help Falling in Love with You" started playing, which is one of our songs. I noticed it was coming from

Spencer and remembered he had bought a new pocket speaker for the beach.

"Oh, cool! Love the new pocket speaker!" I said. He smiled.

We continued to walk, and we came upon rose petals scattered all over the surrounding grass and on the pathway.

"Oh my gosh, Spencer, look! Somebody dropped some rose petals here!"

Spencer stopped underneath a gathering of palm trees and let go of the umbrella, which slowly blew away like something out of a movie. The breeze tossed my long, pink dress.

Then he turned to me, gave me a hug, and whispered in my ear: "I love you so much, Betty. You're my everything."

"I love you too," I replied and hugged him back—still completely oblivious.

"I just couldn't wait any longer," he said as he bent down on one knee.

As I tried to understand what was happening, he reached into his back pocket and pulled out a little white box and opened it.

"Will you marry me?" he asked.

Completely shocked and overwhelmed with emotion, I struggled to get the word *yes* out. We had been talking recently about when we wanted to get engaged, and we both agreed it would be best to wait until my year as Miss America was over. He had completely caught me off guard! And the ring was stunning. I seriously couldn't believe my eyes. We had talked about different ring designs and settings, and I shared what I liked and disliked. He had clearly taken notes because it was beyond perfect. Spencer held me until I recovered from crying. With the tough year I had been having, it was a relief to experience something as happy as this.

Spencer walked me to a little picnic table nearby where he had a bottle of champagne and two champagne flutes waiting for us. He popped the bottle open, and then his sister came out from behind a tree.

"I've got pictures!" she said, holding a camera.

His parents were waiting in the condo, so we grabbed the champagne and headed their way. They cheered when we walked inside, and all of us were excited. They had recorded the whole thing for us from their window.

"So, I'm guessing there's no brunch cruise, huh?" I asked, laughing.

"No," Spencer said. "I had to make something up so you'd get dressed up a bit. I knew you'd kill me if I asked you to marry me when you were wearing a t-shirt and shorts."

My time with Spencer and his family over the next few days was amazing. I couldn't have been more excited to be engaged to the man I loved. Once the vacation was over, though, I had to take off my engagement ring, put it in the little white box, and pretend like it had never happened. I only wore my ring when I was in my hotel room and out of the public eye. It was a tough secret to keep, so you can imagine that the minute Savvy Shields was crowned the new Miss America, I couldn't wait to share my happy news and *finally* wear my ring!

I posted the picture of Spencer and me, showing off my engagement ring on social media as soon as I got backstage and the okay from Alice. From then on, that ring was not coming off my finger for anything! I changed out of my pageant gown and into regular clothes, locked hands with Spencer, and together we walked to a casino to eat pizza. The freedom was glorious.

By morning, the news of our engagement and pictures of my ring were all over social media and pop culture television networks. Our secret was out, and we felt like a celebrity couple! Spencer and I couldn't stop smiling. We headed to the airport and boarded a plane bound for Georgia. A lot of the people on our flight had attended the pageant the night before and recognized me, and I happily took pictures with people on the plane and at baggage claim. But I was even more happy that I was no longer alone. For the past year, I had boarded plane after plane after plane, always sitting by myself. But now I was sitting on a plane next to someone I knew and loved. I was glowing with joy just to hold hands with Spencer and rest my head on his shoulder—and in public no less!

When we got home, I slept for nearly twenty-four hours straight. My entire first week home was probably the most relaxing week of my life. I didn't set a single early-morning alarm. I just laid by the pool and slept as much as I wanted. My new reality without any Miss America pressure was blissful. It was also desperately needed after the whirlwind of the past year. Spencer and I began dreaming about our wedding and what we wanted it to look like. He had been growing out his beard, and I told him, "You definitely have to shave for our wedding day." He agreed and said he would do it for me. We were so excited for our big, fat, Greek wedding one day!

Before my reign had ended, Spencer and I had also discussed him quitting his job as a cop and becoming my new tour manager—booking events, managing contracts, talking to clients, and handling event details. He had already booked several speaking engagements for me, and I loved sharing this exact story (only a much more condensed version!) of how I became Miss America and the importance of being yourself.

We also started traveling back and forth to Nashville to work more closely with Steve Ivey and record music. By December, I released my first song, "Soldier On," which is a dedication to women in the military. Steve suggested Spencer and I move to Nashville for a couple years—at least to get my feet wet in the music industry. Since we were driving there so often, we eventually decided to take Steve's advice, so we moved there in January of 2017. We continued to travel all throughout the country for appearances, and before we knew it, over a year had gone by since my passing on the crown.

Then one day in early November, Spencer's mom, Pamela, told us how Spencer's younger sister and her boyfriend were discussing their own engagement, which was expected to happen soon.

"We've been engaged for more than a year, and we have nothing planned. Are you cool with your little sister getting married before us?" I asked Spencer.

"Yeah, no. I'm not cool with that . . ."

"We need to get married!" I insisted.

"Yeah, we do," he agreed. "We just haven't had time to breathe, much less plan a wedding."

He was right; we'd never been busier. I was speaking constantly and working on my album, which was set to release later that year.

"If you promise me that we'll still have a real wedding one day with family and friends, then we could elope," I suggested.

"Babe. If you're serious, I will shave my beard right now."

"I'm serious," I said. Spencer just wanted to be married; he didn't care about all the wedding stuff.

"We'll still have a real wedding. I promise," he said.

So while Spencer shaved his beard, I found an elopement company that would provide an officiant and a photographer at any

Nashville location of our choice. We booked it, and our nuptials were scheduled to take place in two days' time. That meant we had to get a marriage license the next day, which requires specific documentation, including driver's licenses. I pulled mine out and saw it had expired!

"We'll go to the DMV first thing in the morning, get your license updated, and then get our marriage license," Spencer said.

We woke up extra early to get to the DMV before a long line formed, but of course, there was already a line when we got there. We stood and waited with all the necessary paperwork in hand, or so I thought.

When it was finally our turn, we handed the DMV employee our paperwork.

"We need an original birth certificate," the employee said.

"I don't have that," I said. My heart dropped. "I already have a driver's license," I pleaded. "It just expired."

"We still need original documentation." She wasn't budging.

We walked away unsuccessful. "It's not going to happen, Spencer," I said. "Maybe this is God telling us not to do this."

"This isn't over," he said. "We're going to go to the county clerk and at least *try* to get a marriage license."

Oh no, I thought. "I don't want to get in trouble," I told him.

"We're just gonna try."

When we arrived at the county clerk's office, we had no idea where to go. A security guard holding a sack lunch must have seen the confusion on our faces because he asked us if we needed help. We told him we were there to get a marriage license.

"Oh, follow me," he said. "I'll show you where to go."

We thanked him, and as we followed him to the correct office, we told him we were eloping.

"Man, y'all are doing it right. I wish my wife would have done that with me."

Maybe this is a good sign, I thought. I can't help but look for signs from God in these types of situations.

When we reached the office, he opened the door for us and said, "Alright, blessings to y'all. Have a good day." Then he turned and walked in the opposite direction.

We sat down at the county clerk's desk.

"I need proof of residence and your driver's license," she said. "Who wants to go first?"

"I'll go," I volunteered. I nervously slid my license across her desk, praying she wouldn't say anything about the expiration date. She typed for a bit and then picked up my license, studying it hard. *This is it, here we go,* I thought.

"How do you pronounce your first name?"

"Oh! It's 'Vah-see-lee-key.' It's Greek," I explained.

"That's a pretty name," she said. She handed me back my license and turned to Spencer. "Your turn," she said.

I couldn't believe it. She finished taking our information and printed out our marriage license! I turned to Spencer and smiled.

That night, I spoke with a representative from the elopement company who was helping us select a venue. We didn't know where we wanted to go; all we knew was that we wanted to be outside.

"How about Percy Warner Park?" she suggested.

I Googled it, and it was perfect. We called Steve and his wife, Sandy, and asked if they would be witnesses at our wedding. They enthusiastically agreed.

Then we started stressing about what to wear. We shopped around the mall not knowing what we were looking for. I only knew

I wanted to look somewhat bridal. Then Spencer spotted peacoats in a department store.

"I've always wanted a peacoat. I think I could rock one," he said. "What if I wore a black peacoat, and you wore a white one?"

"Oh, that's awesome!" It wasn't going to be more than fifty degrees outside, so it made perfect sense.

The next morning, November 8, 2017, was our wedding day. I pin curled my hair the night before and woke up extra early to let them down and to have time to perfectly apply my makeup. Then we met Steve, Sandy, the officiant, and the photographer at Percy Warner Park. Fall in Nashville is gorgeous, and this morning was especially stunning. The sun was shining so brightly that the yellow leaves looked like they were glowing. And we were the only people in the park. It was so quiet we could even hear the light breeze blowing as the officiant read a few prayers and we exchanged "I dos." It was the most beautiful, private, and peaceful ceremony.

After the ceremony, Steve and Sandy surprised us with flowers, champagne, and a real cake to cut. We uncorked the champagne, cut the cake, and just enjoyed each other's company. Spencer and I had an hour-long photoshoot with the photographer, and then we ended the morning with Sandy taking a picture of us driving away from the park in Spencer's Toyota Tacoma.

We hadn't told a soul about our plans for a secret elopement, and we were about to burst with excitement. We wanted to share the news with our families, so we quickly packed our bags and drove four hours to Spencer's parents' house in Macon. My mom was visiting with them that night too, and I was a little worried about telling her. She is fiercely traditional, and I knew she wanted a traditional, Greek

Orthodox wedding for us. I didn't want her to be upset or disappointed.

When we walked inside the house, Spencer's parents said they had a surprise for us: a new TV. We told them we had a surprise for them too, and Spencer held up his hand with the black QALO ring we had purchased from Dick's Sporting Goods for the elopement.

His dad, Rick, was the first to notice: "Y'all got married!"

Everyone was thrilled. I could tell my mom was shocked but genuinely happy for us. We all cried and hugged.

"We're still going to have a real wedding, I promise," I assured my mom.

Between my year as Miss America and the following year of constant travel and work, I wanted, and I think on some level even needed, a simple and intimate ceremony. And we just couldn't wait any longer to be married. I'm so happy that we eloped.

"What's holding y'all back from planning your actual wedding?" my mom asked.

"We just don't have the money or the time right now," I told her.

"Well, y'all aren't going to be paying. Your dad and I are paying for it."

"Oh!" I was truly surprised. I respect my parents. After all they had done to support me, I never would have assumed they would pay for our wedding. "Well, that makes a big difference." Spencer and I looked at each other excitedly.

"Let's pick a date," she said. "Tonight!"

"How about March 2019?" I suggested. Spencer and I first met during the month of March.

"Why not March 2018?"

"Mom, that's not even six months away."

"I planned my wedding in six weeks. We can do this!" There was no stopping her. She was going to make sure we had a real wedding.

"Well, I'll ask Father John if March 2018 is available."

I contacted our priest, Father John, from my home church and asked about March. He said that because of Lent, March wasn't an option and suggested April instead. I didn't have any meaningful connection to April, and I'm too sentimental to choose a date without significance. I checked the calendar anyway and saw that the thirteenth of April was a Friday.

Hmm, I thought, *thirteen* is *a significant number in our relationship.* Spencer was born on the thirteenth of December on a Friday; he was number thirteen on a drill team at the Citadel; I was called "Lucky Number Thirteen" at the Miss America pageant, and I was crowned on the thirteenth of September.

"Spencer," I said, "How cool would it be if we got married on Friday the thirteenth?"

"Oh yeah," he said. "That's our wedding date."

I checked with Father John, and he contacted the Metropolis for their approval before texting me back:

> Good news. The Chancellor said that normally
> weddings are not permitted on Fridays in com-
> memoration of Jesus' crucifixion on the cross.
> But because April thirteenth is Bright Friday
> next year, and Bright Friday is the first Friday
> after Pascha, or Easter, the wedding is permitted
> because it's a day of celebration because Jesus
> rose from the dead.

That meant that Friday, April 13, 2018, was the only Friday that the church would permit us to marry that entire year, and it was called "Bright Friday." We were thrilled. I mean, what were the odds of that happening? I took it as a sign from God.

But I was dreading my next conversation with Father John. I had to tell him we were already legally married. I feared he may not be able to perform the traditional, formal, Greek Orthodox ceremony.

"So it was just a civil wedding performed by an officiant?" he asked.

"Yes," I confirmed. "We got a marriage license and had the officiant perform the ceremony."

"That makes no difference at all. The church just considers that a civil union, not a sacrament of matrimony. To the church, you're not married. Legally, you are married, but to the church you're not. We'll still do a full-on wedding ceremony."

Words cannot describe the relief I felt at that moment. With a date secured, the wedding planning was in full swing. Like lots of little girls, I dreamt of my wedding day and made promises to friends throughout my life that they would be part of my special day. We couldn't wait to ask some of our dearest friends and family members to be a part of our bridal party. At first, Spencer wanted fifteen groomsmen.

"Spencer, I don't even know fifteen girls who would stand with me at our wedding!" I was still the girl with only a few but very close friends.

We managed to narrow our bridal party lists down to nine. I had my childhood best friend Natalie, Sophia, Spencer's sister, my first cousin, my best friend from high school, my best friend from college, and my Miss Missouri, Miss Kansas, and Miss Wisconsin sisters from

Miss America. Spencer's groomsmen were mostly high school and Citadel friends but also included my brother, Mikey, and my first cousin's husband.

As we began planning, the TV show *Say Yes to the Dress* reached out to me, and Steve coordinated with them to arrange my appearance on the show. I've been watching *Say Yes to the Dress* forever, so to appear on it was surreal. For lots of girls, picking out a wedding dress is almost as exciting as the wedding day itself, and I was no exception. I only invited my mom, Sophia, my dad, and Spencer's mom, Pamela. I wanted this day to be meaningful, and I didn't want an entire entourage giving me conflicting opinions. By this point in my life, I had worn so many gowns that I couldn't wait to pick something that was completely different and unique.

"We'll know immediately when she finds the dress because of the way she'll walk in it," my mom said. "She'll smile differently and walk more confidently."

I picked out roughly thirty dresses to try on but only made it through four before finding the one. It was a strapless sweetheart dress with an A-line ball gown skirt. The top layer had hand-laid, three-dimensional flowers of all kinds, and the layer underneath was covered in sequins, which made the dress glisten as I walked. I was beaming, and my family knew I had found my dress too. The detail on this gown was so intricate that it was mesmerizing. This was my dream wedding dress. I picked out a veil that extended a foot beyond the train of my gown. I truly felt like a princess.

"Don't try on anymore," my dad said. "You're done." And he was right. We all agreed this was *the* dress.

Our rehearsal dinner took place the night before the wedding. Moving speeches were given by Spencer's best man, my dad, and

Spencer's dad. Even though the bride and groom don't usually give speeches, Spencer and I wanted to thank all the people who had worked tirelessly to make our wedding happen—namely Liz, my mom, and my dad. I also shared a diary entry I had written just a few days after meeting Spencer. I had written three pages about how I already loved him, and the entry ended like this: "I absolutely know Spencer Maxwell will be my future husband. He is the man I want to grow old and have kids with, and I couldn't be more content with that idea."

Just about everyone in the room was crying, especially me. After the rehearsal dinner, we took our bridal party back to Spencer's parents' house for a pool party. As the night came to a close, my brother drove me to the nearby hotel where our guests and my mom were staying. I quietly opened the door to my mom's room and climbed into bed.

I woke up on the morning of my wedding day feeling totally at peace even though I hadn't fallen asleep until 2:30 that morning. We all joked that I was #Bridechilla instead of #Bridezilla. The only thing I was really particular about was not seeing Spencer until I walked down the aisle. That tradition was hugely important to me. But we *did* want to at least visit with each other before the ceremony, so we wore bandanas and met up in the bell tower of the church, which hadn't been renovated since the 1800s. It was breathtaking, even with the beat-up wooden floors and peeling plaster walls. The stained-glass windows let in a soft light, and Spencer and I held hands and prayed together.

The ceremony started, and we didn't use traditional Byzantine music like you would in a Greek Orthodox ceremony. Father John said we could use whatever music we wanted for the procession and the recession. I walked down the aisle to an instrumental version of Ellie Goulding's "Love Me Like You Do" by the Brooklyn Duo, which was another one of mine and Spencer's special songs.

At the climax of the song, the double doors to the church swung open, and my dad and I stepped out into the aisle. Spencer had the ultimate groom's reaction. He broke into tears and nearly fell to his knees, which made it almost impossible for me to keep it together.

It was a perfect ceremony. No one in the bridal party passed out, which was a legitimate concern because Greek Orthodox weddings last forty-five minutes. One of my favorite moments of the entire day was when Spencer leaned over to me during the ceremony and whispered, "I'm converting."

"What?" He was whispering so quietly that I wasn't sure I heard him correctly. He said it again. "Really?!" My heart swelled with emotion. I would have never expected him to do that.

"Yeah," he smiled.

Right after the ceremony, Spencer and I walked down the aisle and into a smaller room to wait while the guests exited the church. I completely broke down inside that room. He held me while I cried, and I just couldn't wrap my head around everything that was happening. This was the best day of my life. I had dreamt of my fairytale dream guy who would one day become my husband, and he was a chump compared to Spencer. I was overcome with gratitude and joy for the life and husband God had given me.

Once we were done taking pictures with the photographer, we boarded a historic Macon trolley and rode to our reception, which proved to be the party of a lifetime. The song for our first dance was called "Sway," and it was a song off my first album that I'd specifically written for Spencer. Then we danced with our parents before changing into our reception outfits. I wore a short, white dress with hand-laid flowers that was similar to my wedding dress, and Spinny wore black shorts with a white, Harley Davidson t-shirt, his tux vest, and a bow tie. We also wore matching Vans high tops: mine were white, of course, and his were black. Together, we had choreographed our own Greek dances, and he was so nervous about performing his that he had been practicing for months. And he nailed it!

After our Greek dances, we went straight into party mode. We danced for hours with our bridal party and guests, and around eleven o'clock that night, the DJ asked, "Can I get Betty on the dance floor?" I made my way to the center. "Alright, Betty, we have a surprise for you. Turn around!"

My family had arranged for the Chick-fil-A cow to show up at my wedding, and now he was waiting to dance with me! Anyone who knows me knows I love Chick-fil-A. It's kinda my thing, and I freaked out. And the cow was wearing a tux—bowtie, top hat, and all! Trays of Chick-fil-A nuggets and cookies were served, and people took pictures with the cow. It was such a fun surprise.

We had to leave the venue at midnight, so everyone who was still partying with us went back to Spencer's parents' house. It was sixty-eight degrees that night, so most of us were in the hot tub, but that didn't stop people from jumping into the pool too. We were having so much fun that Spencer and I didn't even get to bed until 6:30 the next morning.

It would be impossible (and probably boring) to share every amazing detail of my wedding day. It could truly be a book of its own. But thanks to Liz, Spencer and I were a featured couple on *The Knot*, the wedding magazine and website. So if you really want to hear every lovely detail, you can check it out there!

I know how all of this may sound: Betty found the perfect guy, had a fairytale wedding, and now she's living her happily ever after. But Spencer didn't just walk into my life. As the saying goes, I had to kiss a few frogs before finding my Prince Charming. And with those frogs came some tough lessons on love. Those lessons taught me that I needed to be intentional about the qualities I sought in a husband.

Everyone looks for something different when it comes to finding a partner for life; I realize that. But if identifying some of the qualities I looked for spares you even a minute of heartbreak, then maybe what I've learned is worth sharing. Here's how to find your Spinny:

Find "the one." Easier said than done, I know. But this was one of the hardest lessons for me to learn. It's way too tempting to stay in a relationship that isn't working for you when you've invested time into it. But I urge you to never settle. I can't tell you how many times I thought, *Maybe he's the one, but* . . . Listen, if he's the one, you won't start that sentence with "maybe." Don't waste a second more of your life with Mr. Right Now and deliberately pursue "the one." No compromises. No exceptions.

Find a gentleman. Spencer opened the car door for me on our first date and still does. He makes sure I walk on the inside of the sidewalk to distance me from passing cars. When we eat out at a restaurant, he pulls my chair out for me before seating himself. He never skips a beat with his thoughtfulness. Chivalry doesn't have to be dead, and maybe I'm just an old-fashioned Southern girl, but to me, these types of gestures feel respectful and loving.

Find someone who believes in you. When other guys I dated tried to dissuade me from my dreams, I told myself, *He's still a good guy. He just doesn't get it.* Nope. He's not the one. If he is saying those kinds of things to you, then you're settling. There is a guy out there who thinks your dreams are the best and not only believes in you but will also do whatever he can to help you achieve them. Spencer gave up so much to move to Nashville with me and jump into a management role despite having zero experience. That's the kind of support you should expect from a husband, and it's the kind of support you should give him in return.

Find someone who loves his family. If Spencer's family needed help, he's the type of person who would get into his car and meet them wherever they were without a second thought. When his sister attended a debutante ball, he told her how beautiful she looked. On our wedding day, he told his mom, "This is the most beautiful you've ever looked to me." He tells my mom how lovely she is and constantly encourages her to get back into the dating pool. It's sweet and selfless, and it's sincere. He's even bros with my dad, and he's the only guy I ever dated who I could honestly say that about.

Find someone who loves you for exactly who you are. A lot of us fall into a trap where we feel like we can't be ourselves with a guy because he might reject us or love us less. Or we think, *I can only talk about this with my girlfriends.* That's not how it should be. Spencer is the only person I feel I can be my fully goofy self with—weird voices, impressions, and all. My skin can be broken out and my hair a mess, and he still thinks I'm beautiful. Find someone you can share that kind of comfort with—someone with whom you can be completely vulnerable and your fully authentic self. Someone you can communicate with about anything and everything. You should be able to enjoy a certainty that this guy loves you unconditionally.

Find someone who doesn't run from a fight. Some people think that the testament of a good relationship is never fighting. This couldn't be more wrong, in my opinion. When you argue with your spouse, it means you care enough to fight for the relationship instead of holding your feelings inside or walking away. Care enough to hear each other out—even when you don't agree. It's okay to disagree or feel angry as long as you remain respectful to one another and move on. Never hold grudges and always own up to your mistakes. Humble yourself and apologize. After a big fight, no matter what, Spinny will always come to me and apologize if he was in the wrong, and I do the same. Humility and communication are key in a relationship.

Find someone who is God-fearing. When I first met Spencer, I thought, *There's no way this guy is as cool, down to earth, and tatted up as he is* and *godly*. I was so wrong. He follows the Word of God, prays constantly, and encourages my relationship with God. It's important to both of us that our relationship is built first and foremost on the foundation of Christ. Find someone whose spiritual values align with yours and who not only shares your walk in faith but also strengthens it.

There is no perfect marriage or perfect partner. We all make mistakes and can do and say hurtful things sometimes. But I truly believe that if you put God first and your spouse second, you can have a healthy, happy marriage. If you are willing to love your partner as you love yourself, that's half the battle. Spencer and I don't have a perfect marriage. We've been through our fair share of hard times even in the short time we've been married. But we are committed to each other for better or for worse. Unconditionally. Don't ever settle for anything other than that. I promise you, it's worth waiting for.

CHAPTER 11

Life as Mrs. Maxwell

After our big, fat, Greek wedding, Spencer and I returned to Nashville. Our work schedule was jam-packed: I had speaking engagements, singing performances, ceremonies, and fundraisers. I was also booked for hair and makeup gigs for brides and pageant girls. I had started doing hair and makeup tutorials on YouTube and Instagram, and Spencer and I started our own YouTube series called Betty & Spinny. Our followers told us that they loved seeing and hearing us as a couple, so in our YouTube videos, Spencer and I discuss all kinds of different topics and answer questions from followers.

Now, I have to give credit where it's due: Spencer is the creative genius behind the majority of our video content. He's always had a creative side, and before attending the Citadel, he even considered attending Savannah College of Art and Design for filmmaking. He taught himself how to use film-editing software like Final Cut Pro, and he comes up with fresh content ideas all the time. Naturally, he edits our YouTube videos and helps me with my Instagram posts.

Because of work—events, appearances, and whatnot—we decided to save money by delaying our honeymoon, and we started house hunting in Nashville instead. It was more important to us that we settle into a home of our own than take a vacation. Nashville is truly becoming the Los Angeles of the East Coast, so the cost of living is ridiculously high. For three months we looked at house after house but without success. We were having trouble finding a home that we liked that was also within our price range.

Frustrated, we started looking at houses farther out from the city—up to forty-five minutes out. Then we realized that if we were considering living that far from Nashville, why wouldn't we just move back to Georgia? All we really needed was to live within a reasonable distance from the airport, and Nashville would still be within driving distance. And if we settled in Georgia, that would put us closer to our parents, which we definitely wanted for when we eventually have kids. Moving back home to Georgia sounded better and better, so we started our search in Atlanta, but again, we weren't having any luck.

Then one morning in early June, Spencer woke up early and started scrolling through a realty website. He woke me up (too early!) and said, "Check out this house." At first, I rolled my eyes. I don't like to be woken up—especially when I was already feeling defeated by the process. I'd already determined in my mind this was just another house that probably wouldn't work out. Reluctant, I rolled over and scrolled through the pictures anyway. And I loved it. We called Spencer's parents and asked them to check it out since we were still in Nashville. They Facetimed us as they walked through, and it was perfect. We wanted it.

"You need to make an offer right now," Spencer's dad, Rick, said. "Eight other people are outside waiting to see it."

We rushed to put in an offer and waited anxiously. About a week later, we got the news from our realtor that the house was ours! Our boys, Moose and Batman, two teacup Yorkies, would finally have their own yard to run around and play! We finished all the paperwork and closed on the house in late June. I was already scheduled to do hair and makeup at the Miss South Carolina Pageant during that entire week, so Spencer and I had only two days to pack our entire apartment. I'm not sure how we did it, but by the grace of God, we did. Then Spencer hired a moving team to help him load up a U-Haul, and with our Jeep in tow, he drove four and a half hours in the pouring rain from Nashville to our new home. I couldn't wait to finish up in South Carolina and settle into our first home together!

One of the things I loved most about our house was the basement. It was already completely finished and huge. Half of it was one long room with hardwood floors, and I envisioned the space to have a small-scale runway that would be perfect for pageant coaching. I've wanted to get into pageant coaching since becoming part of the community myself. I had experienced some not-so-great coaches—people who tried to change me and mold me into someone I'm not, so I wanted to do just the opposite. I want to help girls grow into the best versions of their authentic selves. From my experience, this type of coach can be hard to find, and if I can be a positive influence and a source of encouragement, then that's exactly what I want to do.

Once we were settled into our home, I started acquiring clients for pageant consultations. I work with girls from all across the country and from all different pageant systems, not just MAO, and I've really come to love it—particularly working on talent. I feel most helpful to singers since we share similar backgrounds, and I've since discovered how much I love staging and choreographing a singing performance.

As usual, Spencer and I were incredibly busy, and by the time Christmas rolled around, we were very much looking forward to going home to Macon. Every year, we spend Christmas Eve with Spencer's dad's side of the family, and then we spend half of Christmas Day with Spencer's family and my mom, and then half of the day with my dad out on the farm where I grew up. Spencer and I were so ready for a break that we even headed down a day earlier than usual for a little extra family time.

The weather the day before Christmas Eve was beautiful, and we spent our time outside with Spencer's parents, laughing and telling stories. Then my mom came over in the evening, and we were getting ready to play a board game. I suddenly realized Spencer and his mom, Pamela, weren't in the room anymore.

When I looked around and didn't see them, I figured Pamela and Spencer were arguing in private. Pamela had been drinking heavily that day, and she and Spencer would often fight whenever she drank. She struggled with mental health issues for years, and her drinking would get out of control at times, but we never thought of her as an alcoholic. My mom and I waited for them for what seemed like forever.

I heard their voices coming from Spencer's parents' bedroom, so I walked back there to check on them. "No, Betty," Spencer said. "Don't come back here."

"Okay. Sorry," I apologized and returned to the living room, assuming they were having a bad one. I didn't want to interfere. It had been over an hour, so I told my mom I didn't think the game was going to happen and suggested she go home since she had to work the next day. She left, and I laid on the couch and waited for Pamela and Spencer.

A considerable amount of time passed, so Rick went into the bedroom to intervene. Shortly after that, Spencer and Rick walked out of the room and then out the back door. Not a minute after they walked outside, I saw Pamela leave the bedroom and walk out the front door, which was strange because she never left the house using the front door—especially around nine o'clock at night. But I didn't think much of it because Spencer and Rick were out back, and I assumed she wanted to avoid them. Then just a few seconds later, I heard a gunshot. Spencer and his dad heard it too, and we all thought maybe it was the neighbors who had a firing range in their backyard.

A few more seconds passed, and I thought it was strange that Pamela hadn't come back into the house. Henry, their goldendoodle, started barking at the front door. My heart started to race, and as much as my mind didn't want to go to the possibility of what may have transpired, I knew something was off and had to check. I stood up and cautiously walked toward the front door, terrified of what I might see. I peeked through the screen door, too afraid to open it all the way. Through the screen, I saw Pamela's legs on the ground. Panic took over my body, and I ran through the house and out the back door to find Spencer and Rick.

"Something's wrong!" I screamed. "Pamela's on the ground!"

We ran through the house and out the front door, but we were too late. She was already gone. The gunshot we heard had been from her.

I couldn't control myself and screamed over and over. Fortunately, Spencer's training as a cop kicked in. He told me to call 911, so I ran back inside to find a phone. I finally found Spencer's, but I was shaking so badly that it took me a minute to unlock it. I'd never had to call 911 before. I didn't know what I was supposed to say. I was crying so hard and felt so confused that I could hardly talk, and yet I was somehow able to communicate clearly to the police. I don't know where the words came from, but I truly feel like they had to be from God.

The 911 operator stayed on the phone with me until the police arrived at the house. While on the phone, I stood against the wall, sobbing and shaking. Then Spencer came into the house, ran up to me, put his hands on my shoulders, and promised me we were going to be okay. I couldn't believe he was even thinking about me. We were all in total shock, and yet Spencer felt compelled to comfort me, his wife, amid the confusion and hurt that swirled around us. I was astounded, but it meant the world to me.

The police arrived quickly, and Spencer called my mom and his brother-in-law and broke the news. My mom, Spencer's sister, and her husband arrived shortly thereafter. The police asked us questions about what happened that night, and when everyone finally left, the three of us sat outside, unable to say much at all.

That night, Spencer and I couldn't sleep. We stayed up just talking and crying. Anyone who knew Pamela knew she loved her kids more than anything. But, like most people who have had too much to drink, she would often say hurtful things she would have never said sober. In between sobs, Spencer said, "I know that wasn't my mom. I know that was Satan. It was the alcohol mixed with her new medications. That's what took her. That was not the mother who raised me."

While we were all in shock over what had happened, we were also aware of her family history. Pamela's own mother had been an alcoholic who had committed suicide when Pamela was only twelve years old. It was a traumatic experience for Pamela, especially since she had been the one to find her mother. Then, years later, after Pamela and Rick married, her brother committed suicide as well. He, too, was an alcoholic, and again, Pamela was the one to find her family member's body.

Shortly after the death of her brother, Pamela learned she was pregnant with Spencer. He was her miracle baby—her everything. As he grew up, it became harder and harder for her to let him go. She was really upset when he left home for the Citadel. She started smoking and drinking to cope, and it seemed like she was trying to fill a void with vices. Spencer is an incredible son who always calls his parents and puts his family first, but Pamela still struggled with his absence.

It was also hard for Pamela when Spencer and I got married. She would cry and tell him she felt like she was losing him. And while Pamela was always kind and loving to me and would literally do anything for me as if I were her own daughter, I admittedly found her reaction frustrating. It seemed like she was struggling to be happy for him, and that was confusing to me. I couldn't understand it.

Initially, all I felt was sadness for Spencer's family. But the more this new reality started to sink in, the more I found myself feeling angry. I was angry with her choice to take her own life immediately after a huge fight between them. Her last words to him were awful, and she said things that no son should ever have to hear from his mother. I was terrified Spencer would blame himself. Spencer and his mom were close, and he was indescribably hurt and sad over her loss. It hurt him in ways I can't possibly understand, and the pain she inflicted upon him honestly enraged me.

Pamela suffered from alcoholism, mental health issues, and unresolved childhood trauma, and even though she took antidepressants and other medicines, she still drank often. And that's when things would take a turn for the worst. For many surviving family members, the knowledge of a family history of suicide can be a source of comfort, but it only made me angrier. Of all people, she knew how suicide affects the survivors. Some of her closest family members had left her, choosing to take their own lives, and she knew that pain better than anyone. Now, she had done it to her own family.

I couldn't wrap my head around why or how she could do this to her own husband and kids. Yes, she struggled at times. We all do. But Pamela was a godly woman. For two years, she had been writing a book of her own about her life experiences because she wanted to help other people see how they, too, can turn to God during hard times. I was deeply confused by her actions. I continued to dwell on my anger, and I honestly started to feel a bitterness boiling inside me. I remember thinking, *I'm going to love Spencer better than that.* I wanted to blame Pamela even though I knew my anger was neither right nor justified.

I didn't know how to deal with so many conflicting feelings. I certainly didn't feel like I could talk to Spencer. She was his mother, so it's not like I could say, "I hate your mom for doing this to you and your family," even though that was exactly how I felt. I wanted so badly to say those words out loud. I didn't know if my reactions and feelings were normal. I had no idea what my role or responsibility was as the wife of someone whose mom chose to take her own life. I tried Googling things like "how to cope with your husband's mother's suicide" and "how to support a spouse whose parent has committed suicide" and couldn't find anything—not a website, book, or any other kind of resource. I knew I wasn't the first wife to have been in such a position, but it sure felt like I was.

I continued to pray hard, but my anger wasn't going away. Spencer sensed something was up with me; he knew something was wrong. "You need to talk to me," he said. "You need to tell me how you're feeling."

"I can't talk to you about this, Spencer."

"You're mad at my mom," he said. "You hate her for doing this."

He had read my mind. Spencer is the only person I know who would listen to someone else talk about their feelings about a tragedy that first and foremost affected him. But he understood that her death affected me deeply too. Even though Pamela wasn't my mother, she was the mother of the person who I love most in the whole world, and he loved her beyond words.

I let it all out. I was so, so angry, and I told him exactly how I was feeling. I shared every ugly thought. I admitted to him that I couldn't believe a mother could do this to her son. I told him I thought she did it for attention, and that she wanted the final word in that argument to make him feel bad for her. After I told him all these things, I realized I had been sobbing and borderline screaming. I knew I was wrong to feel how I did. I knew Satan was trying to get at me and was working hard to pull us apart—to break us. I was ashamed of how I felt because I had never felt such dark feelings in my life.

Spencer understood. I don't know how, but he didn't judge me for how I felt. He just listened. But my brutal honesty also unleashed something in our relationship, and it wasn't good. We were having knock-down, drag-out fights. On top of that, I felt depressed all the time and worried that the loss of his mother would take us down too. I was afraid that now that Pamela was gone, she was going to take Spencer with her. I began to question everything. Would we get past this? Would Spencer allow this to fester and never let it go? Was his mom going to take my place even though she wasn't with us anymore?

Our grief and feelings were still so fresh. I knew there was no way he could be over his mother's death after just a couple of months, but I was so ready for it to be over. I wanted to go back to our normal lives. I wanted him to be focused on me again, and I knew that was the most selfish feeling imaginable. I couldn't stand the possibility that his grief would overtake our marriage and our marriage would fall apart because of what she did. I wanted him to know how much I loved him and that I was still here and would never leave him. I wanted him to turn to me. All the while, I knew how wrong it was for me to feel ready to move on and get back to the way things were before her death.

Spencer can fight so hard, but he also has this amazing ability to let things go. He'd say, "I'm sorry. That was my fault. I obviously don't understand how hard this is for you too." He was willing to own up to his mistakes and apologize, and so was I. After every fight—and there were so, so many of them—we would make up as hard as we fought. We'd cry and come back together, and with every fight, we learned more about each other.

We learned that it's okay to fight. It's important to be honest about your feelings and not bottle them up. If anything, we learned the worst thing you can do is *not* talk about it. I prayed for wisdom and the ability to understand Spencer's perspective because the glaring truth was that it wasn't about me. I had to remind myself that I couldn't be a possessive, overprotective wife. I had to be willing to step into my husband's shoes and meet him wherever he was.

We turned to God and prayed for peace. Only then were we able to find solutions and ways to support each other. There's no way that you can go through something like this and it not affect you—for the good or the bad. I'm so thankful that through this, our marriage has cultivated resilience. And as strange and backward as it must sound, that resilience has been a gift from God. This loss has taught us so much about marriage, about ourselves, and about what really matters.

You're not going to find answers to life's greatest questions through earthly things. You're not going to find answers by festering over details and nursing feelings of anger and resentment. You have to look to God. It would have been so easy to allow myself to feel angry about it forever and hate Pamela for leaving the man I love with a hurt that will never go away. There were times when Spencer would have a sudden breakdown, and I would ask myself all over again, *Why did she do this to him?* In those moments, I had to remind myself that she was not well, and the woman who took her own life was not Pamela. I have to distinguish the alcoholism, depression, and unresolved childhood trauma from the beautiful, loving person who Pamela was. I had to forgive her—not only for the sake of my marriage but also to start my own healing.

In fact, I cannot sufficiently express my gratitude for Pamela. Spencer often says that his future had two paths: he could have become an inmate or a police officer. Both were totally possible. As a child, he was prone to violence. He loved to set things on fire and blow things up. But Spencer will tell you that the reason he chose a more positive path was because of his mom and how she raised him. She taught him to turn to God, and she is why he is the Christian man he is today. His faith has strengthened mine and continues to do so.

We may think we're in control and believe our relationship with God is so strong it's unshakable. But when awful things like this take you by surprise, you can't help but question everything in your life. Satan will find a way to creep into your thoughts, especially during dark times. It's up to you whether or not you let him win. You may want to blame God or turn your back on him. But I'll never forget Spencer's faith the night we lost his mom. He kept saying, "I'm not going to blame God. I'm already praying for his strength. Only through God are we going to get through this."

Today, we are at the place I prayed for us to get to during that dark time. We are back to normal, or at least our new normal. We are able to feel happy again, and that's all because of our faith and Spencer's unbelievable strength to make it through the darkest time of his life. He is the strongest person I've ever known. Despite everything Satan tried to do to tear us apart, we supported each other and made it through the darkness. We are closer for having experienced such profound loss, and our marriage is stronger than ever.

When you experience tragedy or trauma, you can let that awful thing define you, or you can try to make something good out of it. Pamela wanted to help people, and that's what she was going to do with her book. Our decision to share the loss of Spencer's mom in this book and on our YouTube channel was not an easy one, and not everyone supports it. But ultimately, we feel that by sharing our experience, we are not only helping to finish Pamela's work, but we're also helping anyone else who may be suffering through a dark time in their life.

We recognize that our platform gives us a unique opportunity to make a difference in people's lives. We can show others how we continue to turn to God and each other to grow stronger in our faith and in our relationship. Our hope is that this experience will give someone the courage to think, *I can get through this too*. And if sharing this story helps just one person, we feel it's more than worth it.

Suicide affects countless people, yet it's so rarely talked about. And therein lies a huge part of the problem: no one talks about it. Until this happened in our life, I had no idea how many people were affected by this kind of loss. Everyone knows someone who has taken their own life or been profoundly affected by someone who did. People who I have known for years started reaching out to me and sharing their experiences with suicide. So many of their experiences took place years ago—for some when they were just kids—and they're only just now allowing themselves to talk about it.

Nothing can prepare you for the loss of suicide. Nothing can prepare you for the amount of suffering and sadness and questions you will face. Suicide is a scary and uncomfortable subject; I get it. You feel isolated and alone when you're going through this kind of grief. But you can talk about it. You need to talk about it.

And if you are struggling with your own thoughts of suicide, please reach out to someone you trust. If you don't feel like you have anyone, call the National Suicide Prevention Lifeline at 1–800–273–8255. You are not alone, and there are people who love you and want to help you. God's plan for your life isn't to leave you alone in your pain. Reach out to someone.

My first year as Mrs. Maxwell was full of life: joy, excitement, stress, and tremendous grief. I have learned from all of it. Spencer and I went from being excited newlyweds with plans and dreams for our future to navigating a loss that ultimately deepened our marriage and brought us closer together. But it was hard, painful work. And we had to lean on God in a way we never had before. I pray that when heartache happens in your own life, you can do the same. Romans 12:9 says, "Cling to what is good." Look to God. Focus on what really matters. Hold tight to your loved ones. Never take one second for granted. Call your mom. Call your dad. If you're a parent, hold your children. Seek professional help. Discover God's unconditional love and confide in him. He is good, and he always has a plan.

CHAPTER 12

Above All, Be Yourself

One of the questions I'm asked most often is if I regret competing in Miss America. And while it was so, so hard, never in a million years would I take it back. I may not always agree with the organization's leadership and its direction, but even the greatest organizations have flaws. The reason I chose to tell the truth about my year as Miss America and share my experiences is because I hope to see change. I care.

I pray for the organization to secure strong leadership that restores our beloved Miss America to her former glory: beauty, grace, kind-hearted, humble, strong, and well-spoken. Miss America is confident and unapologetically herself in a world that tries to make us all the same. She affects positive change in the world around her. She inspires. She is a real, relatable girl. In short, she's the whole package.

I am proud to be a former Miss America, and I am beyond blessed that God put the Miss America Organization in my life. Being

Miss America was an incredible opportunity that changed my life forever and in so many beautiful ways. Until my year as Miss America, I had no idea I wanted to become a motivational speaker or that I was even capable of such a thing. With that crown on my head, I had a platform, and people listened! I felt a responsibility and a calling to inspire as many young people as possible to follow their dreams, love themselves, *be* themselves, and never give up. This will forever be my message, and I've been able to share it with the world thanks to MAO. And for that, I'm eternally grateful.

Since then, I've found new avenues to spread my message—this book for instance! I also continue to speak at events, write music, coach pageant girls, instruct YouTube tutorials, and film *Betty & Spinny*. I've even started acting and modeling, which I love! I'm finally beginning to live out my passions, and I have God to thank for all of it.

My journey has been and will continue to be full of obstacles, failures, setbacks, and rejection. These things are just parts of life. And mine is certainly far from perfect. At least once a day, I find myself wishing for a social media blackout that would force us to live in the world that existed before Instagram—a world where I wouldn't obsess over posting pretty, perfect pictures 24/7 or be subject to some of the most savage of cyberbullying. The truth is no one's life is perfect, and while most of us know this, it's a truth we all too quickly forget.

I have insecurities, acne, and anxiety. I bite my nails and eat *wayyy* too much candy. And some days, I just don't like the person I see in the mirror. But I'm human! I'm still learning. I'm learning to embrace more natural forms of beauty, and I'm finding the boldness to share it. It wasn't easy to get to this point, and I still have a ways to go. But I refuse to give up. I am perfectly imperfect; *you* are perfectly imperfect, and God loves us that way! Confidence comes so much more easily when we learn to accept that God made us perfectly in his image. Give yourself a chance to love yourself for who you are and not who the world expects you to be. You are enough in God.

Even then, you're still going to have tough days like the rest of us. Your faith and your strength to endure will be tested throughout life, and some days, it will feel impossible—like everything is falling apart. It's okay to feel like a mess, and it's okay to *not* be okay. Whatever you're going through, you are not alone. God is always with you. Don't try to do life on your own! Lean on him, and he will provide everything you need. Give your troubles and sorrows to him, and he will bring you peace and happiness. He will never give up on you, and he makes every moment of your life meaningful. I say this to you because I know; I've been there. I truly believe if you are looking for answers, you'll find them in him.

To go from being a small-town farm girl from rural Georgia to winning Miss America in just a couple of years seemed highly unlikely to say the least. But when I look back, I can see how God prepared me throughout my life for that role and for the things that continue to unfold—both the good and the bad. I may not have all the answers, but God *does*. Whenever I feel lost, I remember that he knows what my future holds, and he is going to give me what I need for each season. And he will do the same for you! Relax in his sovereignty and the knowledge that he goes before you to forge a path and then walks beside you to get you through it. Trust that he is in control and know that he's not finished yet.

And no matter how crazy this world gets, I never want to lose sight of my most important purpose: to honor and serve my Lord and Savior. All God calls us to do is spread his Word and love him, and I try to do that every day. And every day, I feel God working in my life. Ever since I decided to give everything to God, let him lead my life, and bless others with truth from his Word, I have been filled with inexpressible joy. I am so grateful for the blessings I've been given, and I want to bless others by sharing his goodness and love.

Finally, know that there is a beautiful life awaiting you, and the world needs your gifts. The world needs *you*! So take a deep breath and start living your big, beautiful life. Follow your dreams. Be yourself. And never give up.

Choose God. Choose love. Choose happiness.

CHAPTER 13

Lucky #13

Back in chapter 10, I mentioned how the number thirteen carries meaning for both Spencer and me. Spencer was born on December 13; he was number thirteen on a drill team at the Citadel; I was called "Lucky Number Thirteen" at the Miss America pageant; I was crowned on September 13, and finally, we were married on Friday, April 13. So, for a fun bonus chapter, I wanted to share photos from my childhood, pageant years, and beyond. I just couldn't publish a book without pictures in it. And these photos are not just the highlights, my friend, they're a little bit of everything. They capture my life as a farm girl, my awkward tween years (everyone has them), my time as Miss America, my dream wedding, and more. I feel incredibly blessed to have experienced each and every one of these moments, and now I am excited to share them with you! For more photos, check out my Instagram page @realbettymaxwell.

My Papou and Yia Yia Betty.

How beautiful was my Yia Yia?

Mikey and me wearing our German dirndl and lederhosen. I loved wearing that cape even though it was itchy.

Preschool Betty! I always wanted to dress up for school but eventually had to wear a uniform.

Omi holding baby Sophia.

Family photo with our first Great Dane, Jed. He was so well trained that he would bring the phone to my mom when it rang.

Mikey, Sophia, and me by the pool in our backyard. We were in that pool nearly every day during the summer.

Me with our pet deer, Annie, near our treehouse.

I wasn't afraid to hold a dead rattlesnake!

Mom, Dad, and me after I earned a new badge as a Girl Scout Brownie.

Me at my eighth-grade graduation ceremony. I told my mom I wanted my hair styled like Hermione Granger's at the Yule Ball in *Harry Potter and the Goblet of Fire*. My mom nailed it!

My family with Mikey at his high school graduation. I had just started to learn how to straighten my hair, and it clearly wasn't going well.

A backstage photo from when I played the role of Ti Moune in *Once on This Island*. The boy I'm posing with played the lead role opposite me.

Goodbye, high school! I was so happy to graduate.

My family after my very first pageant where I placed first runner-up and won the talent round. This was the dress I borrowed from my Aunt Dodie.

The top five contestants of the 2014 Miss Georgia pageant. I placed second runner-up and won overall talent.

Meet Miss Warner Robins 2015! I was so excited to return to the Miss Georgia pageant and represent my hometown.

The top five contestants of the 2015 Miss Georgia pageant. I won the talent, evening gown, and on-stage question rounds.

Off to Atlantic City! I'm pictured here with my mom (right) and members of the Miss Georgia board (left to right: Greg, Lisa, and Galen).

In Times Square just before my class' appearance on *Good Morning America*. It was also my twenty-first birthday!

My talent performance on the final night of the competition. I was the last one called for the top ten—so nerve-wracking!

This is the look of total shock. I could not believe they were placing the crown on my head.

My first steps down the Miss America runway. My life would never be the same!

Hugging my mom and dad right after I was crowned.

The iconic selfie that Miss America now takes with her entire class after she is crowned.

Posing in the winner's suite at the Taj Mahal Casino Resort with "Team Betty" aka my closest family and friends.

A surreal moment with my Miss America gown. The Sheraton Hotel in Atlantic City displays the gown of each year's winner throughout the entirety of her reign.

I donated a little more than twelve inches of "Miss America hair" to Locks of Love.

En route to another destination during my year as Miss America. I'm wearing Spencer's jacket and clutching a bear he made for Valentine's Day. I always had it on the plane with me.

Doing my best to not freak out while posing with Harrison Ford at the AMAs.

My photoshoot after chopping off my hair. Loved this curly look!

Moments after Spinny popped the question at Siesta Key.

In a sea of US Army soldiers in Kuwait after my performance.

Posing with members of the Navy at the Army/Navy football game where I had just finished singing the national anthem. Definitely one of my favorite photos from the year!

Recording my first album, *Nicotine*, in Nashville. Dreams really do come true!

In my dressing room after passing on the title of Miss America. I could finally post a picture with Spinny and wear my engagement ring. This was the very last picture I took with the crown on my head.

Spinny and I move to Nashville and begin the adventure of our lives!

From our romantic elopement in Nashville's Percy Warner Park.

My home church in Macon, Georgia, on our wedding day.

Just before filming for *Say Yes to the Dress* and picking out my dream wedding gown!

This moment together before the ceremony was so emotional for us.

Spencer didn't care that I wore six-inch heels on our wedding day. He's the best.

Our reception location, Morgan View Farm. God gave us the most beautiful spring day.

Dancing with the Chick-fil-A cow at my wedding reception!

Me and Spencer with his mom, Pamela.

ACKNOWLEDGMENTS

To Spinny: I know for a fact that I wouldn't be where I am today without you. You have given me the support and confidence in myself to have the courage to chase my dreams. You'll never fully understand how thankful I am that God brought you into my life or just how much I love you. You loved me from a distance for a year of our relationship and were loyal and true. Through all the negative things in life, you have remained my constant joy, my truest friend, and my deepest love. I have never doubted us for a second. Thank you for pushing me to follow my heart, for being my manager, and for giving me this fairytale life with you. I love you forever, my Spinny.

To Mom: Thank you for being my mom. It's easy to take everything that a mom does for granted. From being our taxi driver all those years, to supporting every dream I've ever had, to the endless expenses of private school and pageantry. Know that I don't take a single thing for granted. I recognize all you've sacrificed to give me the most incredible life. Thank you for being the best mom ever. I love you.

To Dad: I remember when I was little, people would tell you, "Watch out for that daughter of yours. She's going to be a handful." You would say they were all wrong and they didn't know what they were talking about. You always believed in me. You always pushed me to take the road less traveled. You supported me in everything I did and helped me do better. Thank you for being the coolest dad and for sacrificing so much to give me the coolest life. I am strong and unapologetically myself because of you. I love you.

To Mikey and Soap: Thank y'all for being the absolute chillest siblings in the world. I love that throughout all of the changes and despite the constant craziness in our lives, we've remained loving, mended issues, grown closer, and continue to thrive! I'm so blessed to have y'all in my life. Thank you for always supporting me in every crazy thing I do and for always showing up. I love you.

To Aunt Dodie and Uncle Randy: Thank you for helping me and supporting me in every aspect of my life. Aunt Dodie, thank you for guiding me in the direction of my dreams and for always being there to lend a helping hand. Please know that I feel so blessed to have such an incredible family, and I am forever grateful to you both. I love you!

To Kristy, Keith, Cole, Elijah, Bud, Lisa, Elaine, Bill, Athena, Papou, the Harkins family, the Herrmann family, and the Lekas family: Thank you for always reaching out, sending cards, making phone calls, showing up, being prayer warriors, sending messages, etc. You all mean so much to me and have truly had a huge impact on my life. Thank you for being there for me. I love you.

To the entire Maxwell family: I'll never be able to thank y'all enough for being the most incredible in-laws in the world. I feel so incredibly blessed to call you all my family. You've truly taken care of me during my highs and my lows. Pamela and Rick, you raised the most perfect human being I know, and I promise to always take care of him. I love you.

To Lisa Nulph, Suellen Demaline, Greg Blazer, Galen Kovash, Snooky, Alicia Long, Marcy Waugh, Rodney Johnson, and Chris Taylor: You all are some of my favorite people in the world. You have helped me, molded me, protected me, and supported me in ways that I'll never be able to repay. I love you all so much, and I want you to know that I am a better person because of you. You are all my family, and I love you.

To Liz Brown: I owe you so, so much. You went from being my Miss America tour manager, to my friend, to my family, to my wedding planner extraordinaire. I am so thankful that God put you in my life. You have done so much not just for me but also for my mom, my family, and Spinny. Know that I am forever grateful, Liz. I love you.

To Natalie, Savanna, Rosalie, Hannah, Kensie, Troyano, Savvy, and Victoria: Thank you for being there for me. Thank you for standing up for me and always having my back no matter what. Thank you for supporting my wild dreams and loving me through it. I'm so, so blessed to have friends like you.

To my Miss America class: I am so blessed to have been part of the Miss America class of 2016. I want to say again that I truly believe that any of you would have been a perfect Miss America, and I am honored to have been given the opportunity to represent you all. I love that we still try to keep in touch, and that we support each other as we move forward with our lives. Know that I love y'all, and our time together in Atlantic City will always be some of my most cherished memories.

To Steve and Sandy Ivey: Y'all have become family to me and Spinny, and we have so much to thank you for. Thank you for standing witness at our elopement. Thank you for supporting and believing in me. Thank you for taking the time to build me and my brand into what it is today. You have been there for us during our ups and downs. We truly wouldn't be where we are today without your help and guidance. Forever blessed that y'all walked into our lives. We love you.

To BroadStreet Publishing, Nina, David, Suzanne, and Carlton: Thank you for believing in my story. Thank you for seeing the real me and believing I was worth it. Thank you for your patience and for listening and taking the time to perfect my words so that they may help and inspire others. Thank you for believing in the power of my message and for preserving it in the pages of this book. Endless thanks and all my love.